Doing the Eucharist

HERE'S TO THE GIRLS!

Frances and Sherry and Patricia and Virginia
and Marybelle and Ruth

# Doing the Eucharist
# A Guide to Trial Use

by

DAVID E. BABIN

MOREHOUSE-BARLOW CO.

NEW YORK

# CONTENTS


*Preface*                                          9

1. Liturgy on Trial

   The Principles of Trial Use              15
   Some Criteria                            20

2. The First and Second Services

   The Two Rites                            29
   Eucharist, Celebration, Liturgy          34
   A New Style of Rubric                    42
   The Opening of the Liturgy               47
   Proclamation of The Word                 51
   The Creed                                59
   A Flexible Arrangement                   62
   The Penitential Order                    64
   Intercessory Prayers                     68
   Exchanging the Peace                     74
   Summary                                  78

3. The First and Second Services—Continued

   Structure of the Second Part             80
   The Offertory                            83
   The Great Thanksgiving                   87
   Fraction and Communion                   94
   Thanksgiving and Dismissal               99

4. The Order of Celebration

The Shape of the Liturgy 104
People and Priest: Gather 106
Proclaim and Respond 108
Pray, Exchange, Prepare 110
Make, Break, Eat and Drink 113
Preparing for the Celebration 114

5. Making Use of Trial Use 117

*A Personal Postscript* 123

Article X:

"... the General Convention may at any one meeting ...

(b) Authorize for trial use throughout this Church, as an alternative at any time or times to the established Book of Common Prayer or to any section or Office thereof, a proposed revision of the whole Book or of any portion thereof, duly undertaken by the General Convention.

——*Constitution and Canons* of The Episcopal Church.

# PREFACE

ACTING UNDER the constitutional authority of Article X, the Sixty-second General Convention, meeting in 1967, authorized a new eucharistic rite for a trial-use period of three years. The new rite[1] did not change nor supplant the one provided in *The Book of Common Prayer*. Rather, for the first time in our history, every diocese, congregation, and individual in the Episcopal Church was given the opportunity to experience a new way of doing the liturgy *before* it was promulgated as "The Official" rite of the Church.

As soon as the new service was accepted for trial use, the Standing Liturgical Commission (which had been responsible for drafting and proposing the rite) set in motion some rather elaborate plans to receive reactions from individuals and groups who participated in the trial of this material. The Commission drew up a set of questionnaires to be distributed to all

---

[1] Rite is defined by the dictionary as: "A prescribed form or manner governing the words or actions for a ceremony . . . the liturgy of a church . . . a ceremonial act or action." In the glossary of *The American Prayer Book,* E. L. Parsons and B. H. Jones define rite as: "the prescribed order for the performance of a public service; or . . . such service as actually performed . . . comprising the order of the text as well as of the action and approximating the meaning of *liturgy* or *ritual*." In *The Oxford American Prayer Book Commentary* Massey Shepherd says: "In strict usage the word 'rite' refers to the text of a liturgy, 'ceremony' to the manner of its performance. But," he admits, "the two terms are evidently synonymous on the title page [of the Prayer Book]." We shall use the term as defined by the dictionary and Parsons and Jones and as evidently intended by the Prayer Book; *i.e.,* a formulary which includes both text and directions for the performance of the liturgy.

congregations and to each participating communicant. A network of diocesan and parochial Liturgical Committee Chairmen was established to receive, collate, and forward the replies.

At the same time, the Commission itself began work on revision of the 1967 rite. A sub-committee was established consisting of eleven persons (clergy and lay, men and women) and charged with the responsibility of receiving the questionnaires as they were returned and responding to them by drafting either a revision of the 1967 rite, or a totally new rite, or both, in the light of those replies. In addition to the drafting committee proper, a group of over 250 Consultants, broadly representative of the Church, was recruited. These Consultants were to receive all the reports and interim work of the Drafting Committee as it proceeded and respond with their opinions of the work at each stage of development, in addition to submitting their own ideas. The consultant group was strengthened by the addition of all Chairmen of the diocesan liturgical committees, members of those committees, and the Bishops of the Church. Thus a total of approximately 500 people would be in on every phase of the work of revising existing materials and drafting new ones.

Americans have a sort of innate distrust of any national administrative machinery. It still comes as a surprise to many Episcopalians (as it did even to some members of the drafting committee) that all those thousands of questionnaires on the 1967 rite actually were read by someone at the top and, even more surprisingly, really taken into account in the work of the committee. But that *is* what happened. An enormous amount of time was expended in reading both the questionnaires and the letters that either accompanied them or were sent instead. The time was not wasted. The questionnaires and other communications provided a great deal of information and insight. Most respondents took the matter quite seriously, and many had constructive and helpful suggestions.

The most immediate result of all this was a Schedule of Variations and Substitutions to be applied to the 1967 rite. The Schedule was proposed by the Standing Liturgical Commission and authorized by the Special General Convention II, 1969. Meanwhile, the drafting committee was proceeding with work on new materials. Ultimately, their work culminated in three new rites or, more precisely, two rites and an Order of service. The new materials that were authorized for trial use by the Sixty-Third General Convention meeting in Houston in October, 1970, are the occasion for this writing.

The Standing Liturgical Commission further proposed, and General Convention authorized, extension of the trial use period for the rite approved in 1967. Trial use does not, however, abrogate the official status of the 1928 rite as found in *The Book of Common Prayer*. And so, on any given occasion of a celebration of the Holy Eucharist, we now find ourselves in the position of being able to choose between five basic formularies. Each of them offers a number of possibilities for variation.

The situation looks more confusing on paper than it actually works out to be in practice, for perhaps the most striking feature about the several rites now authorized for trial use is not their differences—although those are real enough—but their structural similarity. Because the formularies are all designed to provide maximum flexibility, differences in the way various congregations celebrate the same rite are likely to be more obvious than differences between the several rites as celebrated in the same parish at various times.

When the 1967 rite was published, under the title *The Liturgy of The Lord's Supper,* it was found that a study manual designed especially for the lay worshipper was a helpful resource and guide to the new worship experience. The present book is intended to do for the 1970 rites what my *Introduction to The Liturgy of The Lord's Supper*[2] did for the earlier trial-use formulary.

As noted, the 1967 rite is still in a period of trial use. Furthermore, for many readers this may be among the first books they have read concerning the liturgical developments taking place within the Episcopal Church. Therefore, I have not hesitated to use material from *Introduction* where it seemed appropriate. Occasionally some of this material has been reproduced exactly as it appeared earlier; more frequently it has been considerably re-worked to take account of a new situation. On the other hand, the present volume is not intended to be merely a revised and enlarged edition of *Introduction.* By far the larger percentage of it is new. If former readers recognize some portions as being familiar, I can only hope they will feel those parts were worthy of repetition.

---

[2] Morehouse-Barlow Co., 1968.

Generally, we will concentrate on the 1970 materials, referring to the 1967 and 1928 (BCP) rites only to point out significant similarities or variations. After over forty years of living with the 1928 rite, it hardly seems necessary to provide an "Introduction" to it or to add to the distinguished list of competent commentaries already in print.

Finally, every worshipper is encouraged to study carefully the introductory essays in *Prayer Book Studies XVII* (1967) and *21* (1970).[3] These careful and helpful papers by the Standing Liturgical Commission provide basic resource material for even a cursory study of the several rites. The present volume is not intended to replace those primary documents. Our goal is to convey something of the tone or feel or spirit of the liturgy itself and of the several ways of celebrating that liturgy in accordance with the new rites. We will study the formularies chiefly as an aid to enriching our experience of worship.

---

[3] The series of Prayer Book Studies is published by the Church Hymnal Corporation, New York. After 1967, the style of numbering these Studies was changed from Roman numerals to Arabic.

# CHAPTER 1

# *Liturgy on Trial*

"In our day there is wide experimentation in liturgical usage. This is merely the expression of the need for liturgical growth. The experimentation should be carried out in seminaries, colleges, and parish churches; but the experiments should be authorized and be duly under the authority of the Church. In this way, the actual working value of the new forms can be tested, mistakes and false methods avoided. After the results are known, then the Church, through her official councils, can decide as to the practical success of the new forms."

THE ABOVE IS, of course, a statement of the principles of trial use and sounds as though it might have been uttered by some member of our Standing Liturgical Commission during the debate over Article X of our Constitution several years ago. As a matter of fact, it is from the pen of Richard Hooker, one of the great Anglican Divines, and is a quotation from his *Theology of Common Prayer,* published nearly four hundred years ago.

With the exception of minor instances and very occasional situations, Hooker's advice was never heeded. In fact, it was not until the 1960's that the Episcopal Church in America got around to adopting the principle that liturgical forms must be lived with, over a period of time and in a variety of circumstances, before one could dare say that they should be officially adopted by the Church as a norm. The whole concept of trial use is a new one for us. Always in the past some committee has drafted a revision of the liturgical rites and proposed them to General Convention. If General Convention was convinced that a revision was desirable, they would (usually after much debate, often stretching over several Conventions) adopt such a revision—which might, or might not, resemble the one originally proposed. Then, in a second Convention, that action was ratified and the change authorized in *The Book of Common Prayer*. Prior to that final authorization, use of the proposed revision was illegal; after action by the Convention, the new formulary was mandatory. In the meantime, few people except those who had attended the Conventions had any real knowledge of the proposed changes. The first thing most Churchmen would know of them would be when they showed up for service some Sunday morning to be told that they would henceforth worship according to the new formularies and that their old Prayer Books were now obsolete.

Those days, fortunately, are gone forever. Under trial use, every congregation and every communicant of the Episcopal Church has an opportunity to become familiar with the proposals *before* they are adopted. We can study them in some depth, we can experience worshipping according to the proposed rites in a variety of settings and situations and over a significant period of time. Finally, we are invited to make known to the Liturgical Commission our reactions, suggestions, criticisms; and recent experience has proven that this is a sincere invitation and that our voices will be heard and heeded.

But the opportunity carries with it a heavy responsibility as well. For democracy to work, it must be practiced. For trial use to succeed as a method of enabling liturgical growth, it must have the widest possible participation. Furthermore, the trial rites should be used over a period of time long enough for the unfamiliarity to wear off; only then will we be in a position to offer a considered judgment. General Convention has placed this responsibility squarely on our shoulders. It is an awesome one indeed, for the Episcopal Church is made up of over three million people, gathered in thousands of congregations large and small, urban and rural, rich and poor, and spans an almost unbelievable variety of worship practices and traditions.

Most of us will feel totally inadequate to meet such a challenge. Some of us have literally grown up with the 1928 Prayer Book and have no other experience by which to judge any liturgical expression. Others have come to the Episcopal Church because of, or in spite of, its liturgy. In either event, most of us have been nurtured on the concept of "our incomparable liturgy." We are apt to approach the consideration of any different liturgical expression with an attitude similar to that of the man in an art gallery: "I do not know anything about art, but I know what I like."

The difficulty with such a thoroughly subjective approach is that "what I like" is notoriously untrustworthy as a standard of judgment. "What I like" changes from time to time in an unpredictable fashion. It changes with my mood, with my physical condition, with my age, and is even conditioned by my companions, by my last meal, and by many unrecognized factors. A liturgical expression such as those we are being asked to consider is something we will have to live with week after week, year after year; therefore, it has to be built of more solid, stable stuff than "what I like."

One purpose of this handbook is to provide some resources for the formulation of a more substantial standard of judgment. It seeks to introduce the new rites and to help the reader arrive at some basis for evaluating the Convention's proposal. At the same time, it must be emphasized that no amount of study can provide an adequate basis for the judgment of any liturgical expression. That is why the Convention did not simply assign the task to a committee of liturgical scholars and then promulgate the results of their work. A liturgy must be experienced, not merely once, on a sort of experimental basis, but regularly, over a period of time sufficient to let it "settle in," "pack down," and have the opportunity to reflect and inform the varying moods and situations of the worshipping community. Without such an experience, we are apt to find ourselves in the opposite situation of the art critic who says: "I know all there is to know about art, but I do not know what I like!" His condition is no more desirable than that of the naive gallery-visitor.

The task of providing an adequate trial use and

submitting ourselves to it is an exciting prospect for many. For many others, however, it is a vexing and frustrating ordeal. We do not lightly alter years of habit; we do not easily change our patterns of worship. It must be kept in mind, however, that we are not at this time being asked to *change*—we are being asked to give fair consideration to the possibility of change. Even this is difficult, of course. Still, the exercise may prove to be valuable for some unsuspected reasons. Robert Hovda has pointed out in *The Manual of Celebration*[1] that "the human race is congenitally idolatrous. We absolutize our rules, our laws, our habits, forgetting the purpose for which they were originally invented and elaborated. To be aware of this tendency in ourselves—and to fight it—is as important as the virtue of obedience."

There is another reason for embracing the practice of trial use: what sociologists call "enlightened self-interest." We are finally becoming aware of the fact that change is not merely desirable or undesirable—it is inevitable and inexorable. The liturgy is not merely a document contained in a book, it is a thing to be lived—a living thing itself. Like all living things, it *will* develop and grow and change. We may stand still and be spectators as the changes roll over and past us while we weep in frustration and curse in anger. Or we may—thanks to trial use—become a part of the process and help to direct and control change so that it is creative rather than destructive.[2]

---

[1] The Liturgical Conference, 1970.

[2] For a more thorough examination of the relation between liturgy and change, see my *Celebration of Life* (Morehouse-Barlow, 1969).

This is the opportunity, and the obligation, given to us by trial use. For the first time, our forms of liturgical worship are not being *im*posed, they are being *pro*posed. The church's rites are not being "handed down from above"; they are being nurtured from the grass roots. At the same time, we should be aware that the rites we are now being asked to consider are not intended to be the ultimate in liturgical formularies. Many people, perhaps a great majority, will find in them a meaningful expression for today. But tomorrow they will need revision to meet the needs and tastes of tomorrow's Christians. Tomorrows are coming at us more rapidly all the time, and we can no longer afford the wasted time of trying—vainly—to bind tomorrow's generations with today's norms. Neither can we afford to circumvent our own responsibilities by relying upon the norms and forms of preceding generations. As our Lord made abundantly clear, our primary responsibility is certainly not for yesterday, nor is it for tomorrow. Our basic obligation is to today.

The liturgy for the Holy Eucharist is not the only material undergoing trial use. Indeed, General Convention has authorized trial use of suggested revisions for just about all of the Prayer Book. In the various *Prayer Book Studies* we find new formularies for the celebration of Christian Initiation, Holy Matrimony, Ordination, Burial, the Daily Office, and virtually every other service commonly known in the Episcopal Church as well as the addition of some forms of worship unfamiliar to many. Here, we will focus our attention exclusively on the rites for celebrating the Holy Eucharist; but before we proceed it would be well to establish some criteria.

In *Introduction to The Liturgy of The Lord's Supper* some criteria were proposed by which any liturgical expression might be judged. The list was only partial and tentative, yet it proved helpful to many. For that reason, it is repeated here—with some significant alterations and additions that have been suggested by readers and students. It is still suggestive rather than definitive, partial rather than exhaustive. Even so, it will become increasingly apparent why a valid judgment cannot be made solely on the basis of reading and study. At the same time, it will also become increasingly obvious that an informed, responsible approach to the experience of living the liturgy will put our judgment on much more solid ground than naive experience alone can provide.

A good liturgical form is, first of all, a corporate expression of the total life of the community—at least, it must be capable of carrying such an expression. A good liturgy will be capable of reflecting, offering, and informing all of life. The reflection must be a true one, as contrasted to a distorted image. As a mirror, it should be flawless, unbroken, and unclouded, so that the reflection will be true, whole, and clear. A sound liturgy will not force us to pretend that life is other than it really is. It will not force us, coerce us, or even allow us to take refuge in sham or pretense. It will reflect the true nature of man: as created, sinful, redeemed; as dying; and as raised to new life.

Then, in and through the liturgy, we (as individuals and as the community) must be able to offer all of life—honestly. A good liturgy will be able to accept and to offer the totality of our life: the bad as well as the good, the dirty with the clean, the grief and the joy. It must be able to accept the material stuff of our life as a true offering, accepting it for what it really is without having to cover or dress it up to hide its reality. For instance, money is money; it is basic, substantial, common. If this is part of our offering (and if we are going to offer the real things of our life, certainly money will be a part of that offering), then it must be acceptable as money, without apology, embarrassment, or the need to hide its nakedness. In addition to material things, we should be able to offer through the liturgy our true thoughts and feelings, our actions, our very selves and true identities. We dare to make such an offering only if the liturgical form is obviously capable of accepting it and of acting as the medium through which our offering can be made to God.

In turn, the liturgy should be able to inform all of life, realistically. It must be capable of being a medium through which God can act on our lives. It should, therefore, speak to and inspire and enthuse all of life as it really is. If it fulfills this role honestly, the liturgy will not burden us with impossible and irrelevant commands, which lead only to more deeply repressed guilt.

Thus, the circle is completed, and we can see the interrelationship between reflecting, offering, and informing all of life. Perhaps these three form one criterion for the judgment of a liturgy, rather than separate standards. In any event, we find that all this is a pretty tall order, and it should be obvious that no single liturgical expression could possibly meet this ideal fully at any given time. The limitation, however, should be more that of the participants than of the liturgy itself. The better the liturgy, the more receptive it will be to all that we can pour into it; furthermore, this very receptivity or capability will encourage us constantly to pour more and more into it and to be willing to receive more and more from it.

Another important criterion for any good liturgical expression is that it be based upon, and reflect in its words and in its action, sound theology; that is, the liturgy should both say and act what we really believe. Often it is tempting to include in a liturgical form some piece of ceremonial because it is pretty or solemn or convenient, or for some other reason, when as a matter of fact the implications of that ceremony actually deny what the Church professes to be true, or they seem to imply something the Church denies. We are particularly prone to fall into this trap when it comes to ceremonial surrounding the Consecration in the Holy Eucharist. Although the Prayer Book and other Anglican formularies have always been careful to teach a doctrine of the Real Presence of Christ in the Eucharistic action that specifically denies any particular moment of consecration or any particular verbal formula as essential, many of our ceremonies would seem to reject the sufficiency of this Anglican doctrine.

Moreover, any words or actions that would tend to negate the "once, for all time, for all men" character of God's redeeming act in Christ would be bad liturgy because it is bad theology. No matter how "meaningful" it may be, or appear to be, we must reject any rites or ceremonies that would seem to indicate that man earns his own salvation by persuading or influencing God. Sound liturgy *clearly* reflects true theology.

Similarly, a good liturgical form will speak clearly and truly of the mission of the Church. In this regard it will do several things: it will reflect the true purpose of the Body. It will honestly answer the questions: "What are we for?" and "Why are we here?" Secondly, it will challenge the Body to fulfill that purpose, to be about the mission, and thereby to become what it is. And finally, it will provide the support necessary for the Body to fulfill its purpose, for it both to be and to become. Thus, a sound liturgy will speak of purpose, mission, and fulfillment—proclaiming, challenging, and supporting as three facets of a single jewel.

Theoretically, the perfect liturgy would be flexible enough to adapt itself to the many different and ever-changing circumstances of the various congregations of worshippers who will use it. It would be equally at home in the great cathedral and the rural mission. The mission congregation would not be made to feel that they must strive to emulate the cathedral, nor the cathedral congregation feel that they were condescending to do what their less exalted brothers were doing. The ideal liturgy would be adaptable to midweek services for the priest and three of the faithful, as well as to a glorious Easter celebration with choir, orchestra, bulging church, and an episcopal visitation. It would do its job around the hood of a jeep on a foreign battlefield, at the bedside of the dying, at a marriage and at a burial, around the dinner table in a neighborhood "house church," and on the foreman's desk in an industrial plant. And in the parish church, week after week, summer and winter, feast days and fast, on the Fifteenth Sunday after Trinity as well as on Whitsunday, the liturgy will continue to be a meaningful, corporate expression of the life of the Body, a medium through which God can act and the people can respond with all their being . . . and becoming.

Certainly one function of any liturgy has to do with communication. The intended communication is on several levels at once: between the individual participants themselves, between those particular people and all mankind, between those present and those who have been present and have formed our heritage and still remain a part of our corporate consciousness, and between the participants—individually and corporately—and God. This function is so paramount that the eucharistic liturgy is commonly given the title "The Communion." But a good liturgy will not only be *The* communion itself, it will also be a *means* to communion; that is, it will be both the creative act as well as a part of the result. In addition, it will serve as an agent, enabling the participants to enter into the communicative act on all the various levels mentioned above.

Finally, although not strictly criteria for the judgment of a liturgy, there are at least three sets of tensions which any good liturgical expression will seek to reflect and hold in precarious balance. First of all, there is the tension between the traditional and the contemporary forms of expression. Anthropologist

Margaret Mead described that tension quite well in a
paper delivered before the 1963 New York Liturgical
Conference:[3]

> [A liturgy] has to be old, because otherwise it isn't
> polished. It has to be old, because otherwise it won't
> have had enough imagination expended on it. It has to
> be old to be available to everyone born within that
> tradition. But it must be fresh enough so that it can
> continually contain new vision and changed vision
> . . . to use old symbols, but use them anew, to free
> them and ourselves of rigidity and stagnation.

In the same address, Dr Mead pointed out that a
liturgy also must be rich enough to allow for fullness
of expression, but not so rich and elaborate that one
becomes smothered by it. Robert Hovda, in the book
quoted earlier, points out the need "to learn to discern the thread of an organic and living tradition in
liturgical practice and to distinguish this from all
the customs and habits and ways we have inherited
which counter or diminish the tradition. Genuine tradition does not erode or weaken our freedom to
create a liturgy for now. Like good education, it sup-
ports our freedom with the historical experience of the
community."

Another tension held by a good liturgical expression is that between the extent to which the liturgy
expresses and reflects "where the people are" on the
one hand, and the extent to which it attempts to edu-
cate them to something higher, raise their sights, and

---

[3] Reprinted by Forward Movement Publications under the title:
*Ritual Expressions of the Cosmic Sense.*

lead them on to wider horizons on the other. There is always the unresolved question: "Should the liturgy grow naturally out of the lives of the people, or should it be somewhat in the forefront, leading, stretching, challenging them?"

And finally, the good liturgy will reflect the ever-present tension of the Church itself between what we are and what we are becoming in the Body of Christ. We are the company of the saved, while working out our salvation in fear and trembling. The Kingdom of God is coming—yet is in the midst of us. We are—but not yet.

We might translate all these various criteria into a set of questions to ask of a liturgical formulary:

1. Is it honest?
    a) Does it deal with life honestly and realistically, or is it merely an exercise in "playing church"?
    b) Does it allow *me* to be honest and demand that honesty of me?
2. Does it proclaim the purpose (mission) of the Body?
    a) Does it challenge the Body to fulfill that purpose—to become?
    b) Does it provide the resources and the support necessary for the Body to be and to become?
3. Does it serve both as an enabling agent for communication, an act of communication, and as a part of the communication?
4. Are the various tensions actually recognized and

held in balance, or has one side of truth been emphasized at the expense of another?

5. Is it adaptable to the varying circumstances in which it must be used?

Answers to questions of this sort will not be immediately apparent. Any evaluation of a liturgical rite, however, should make an attempt to deal frankly with these issues. Hence the need for informed experience before presuming to make anything more than a tentative judgment.

As indicated above, this list of criteria is merely indicative rather than exhaustive. It should serve, nevertheless, as a good starting point when we undertake to make a judgment of any liturgical expression and it should provide a basis for our further examination of the eucharistic rites authorized for trial use.

One thing, at least, should be quite clear by this time: it is highly improbable that any single formulary will be able to meet all these criteria unless it embodies a degree of flexibility hitherto denied to most rites. The concept of liturgical pluriformity, while of ancient origin and long tradition, is nonetheless new to our generation. Acceptance of it will require an openness of mind and spirit—but openness is, after all, the only path to growth.

CHAPTER 2

# *The First and Second Services*

THE MOST STRIKING feature about the trial-use materials for the Holy Eucharist is that we are being offered not merely one rite, as has always been the case in the past, but three forms for eucharistic celebration. Furthermore, these do not supplant the 1967 *Liturgy of The Lord's Supper* which retains its trial-use status along with the Variations adopted in 1969. Of the new materials, the first two (in order of their appearance in the book) are complete rites. Although they share a common title, they are respectively designated by the simple headings: "First Service" and "Second Service." The third form is given its own descriptive title: "An Order For Celebrating the Holy Eucharist." Because this "Order" is of a somewhat different nature from the two "Services," we shall examine it separately. On the other hand, it would seem to be helpful to look at the First and Second Services side-by-side for comparison and contrast, pointing out at the same time similarities and differences between these new rites and that of 1967. However, each of these two Services deserves at least a brief introduction by way of explanation and rationale.

29

Reactions to the 1967 rite fell roughly into three categories:

1) Those who were opposed to any substantive change in the 1928 version, especially to changes in the language.
2) Those who felt that the proposed revision did not go far enough in making substantive changes, especially with regard to the language.
3) Those who were satisfied that it was a good compromise or intermediate step and would serve well for the present.

Responses that could be classified as either (1) or (2) above were virtually equal in number, and both of them represented substantial portions of the Church. It would, of course, be impossible to draft a single rite that would satisfy both. The decision of the Liturgical Commission was to prepare two Services, thus acknowledging their responsibility to serve the whole Church. At the same time, those who felt that the 1967 rite was acceptable for the present would be accommodated by retaining the trial-use status for that formulary.

One feature of the 1967 rite received overwhelming approval from all sides: the structure or order of the service. We will look at that structure more carefully as we proceed; meanwhile, we can note that it was the broad agreement on this matter that made it possible for the drafting committee to formulate two rites with different styles and unique features in each but which, nevertheless, could be easily recognized as the same liturgy. In spite of their differences, then, the two Services (indeed, all the eucharistic rites under trial use) are obviously intended to *do* the same things. The differences are chiefly a matter of tone or taste, reflecting the same theology and accomplishing the same liturgical action.

FIRST SERVICE: Taking only a quick first glance, many Episcopalians are apt to respond, "So what's the big change?" They will notice that headings have been provided for the various sections and that the material has been arranged on the pages for easier reading and following, but the words appear to be exactly the same as in the 1928 version we are used to. In fact, most of them are.

In effect, the First Service is the rite of *The Book of Common Prayer,* arranged to conform with the order of the 1967 proposal. The most noticeable re-arrangement, and one that is widely applauded by even staunch defenders of the Prayer Book rite, is the positioning of the Prayer For Christ's Church and the penitential material before the Offertory rather than after it. Otherwise, things appear to be pretty much the same.

Actually, the changes are more extensive than that, as we will later point out in detail. But the intention of this rite was to preserve as nearly as possible the "feel" of the Prayer Book. For the most part, it simply reproduces the language of the prayers. There are several prominent linguistic changes that are intended to remove ambiguities, to clarify, or to make unison recital flow more smoothly, but even these have been made within the vocabulary of the original and with the intention of maintaining the integrity of style that characterizes the 1928 version.

For much of this phase of the work, including the beautiful Exhortation appended to the First Service, the Church is indebted to the late Henry N. Hancock, Dean of St Mark's Cathedral, Minneapolis, Minnesota. Dean Hancock so loved *The Book of Common Prayer,* and was so steeped in its majestic language, that he just naturally spoke "Cranmerian English." Yet he was every bit a man of his time.

Thus, the flavor of the Prayer Book permeates the First Service while at the same time the whole rite is informed and enriched by a modern understanding of the liturgical action.

SECOND SERVICE: While adhering faithfully to the basic structure common to all the trial-use rites, the Second Service differs considerably from the First in its language. This is not simply an attempt to render the familiar prayers in a modern vocabulary; it goes deeper than that. Much of the older material is recast into a contemporary mode with an integrity of its own. The syntax, grammar, thought patterns, sentence and paragraph structures—the whole of what is called "style"—are intended to reflect a contemporary manner of expression. However, it is important to note that the Second Service does not drop to the lowest common denominator or resort to slang. There is an important distinction to be drawn between conversational usage (even the most formal conversation) and the language of good literature. This rite is cast in the latter of these modes.

In addition, the Second Service introduces some

new materials to our way of celebrating the Eucharist, as well as some new ways of handling older materials. These, too, we shall look at in some detail.

But the differences between the two services are not explained by attempting to describe them as "merely verbal." Modern communication theory has taught us something of the power of words—a power not only to convey content, but to determine mood, affect feelings, arouse emotions, and even influence the *way* we understand as well as *what* we understand. Leonardo da Vinci and Pablo Picasso both painted pictures depicting the Last Supper. Both are masterpieces. But no one who has ever seen the two paintings could say that his experience of each was the same. In the same way, listening to a Sousa march played by a concert orchestra in an auditorium is one experience; hearing the same music played by a marching band on a football field at halftime is another sort of experience. This is not to say that one is "better" than the other; it is to say that they are not the same. Perhaps Marshall McLuhan goes too far in his insistence that the medium is the message, but surely the medium is a significant part of that message.

The contrast between the different media can only be suggested by our study here. Its full impact will come only with a whole-hearted participation in each of the two services. On the other hand, the difference can easily be over-drawn, for, again, it is chiefly a difference in mood or feel rather than one of content, theology, or intention. In its prefatory remarks, the Liturgical Commission is careful to state that "each of the services is as completely and truly a Eucharist as any of the others, or as any other authorized liturgy of the Church that has been celebrated in its history." The services are offered for the entire Church, and it is not intended that any given congregation devote the period of trial use to the exclusive use of any one of them over the others. The Commission points out that "this implies a certain responsibility on the part of all types of congregations . . . to make use of all the orders, to study them thoroughly, to consider them thoughtfully, and to experiment reverently with each of them."

As we become increasingly familiar with the new rites, no doubt we will come to feel that one of them would be more appropriate to a particular occasion than any of the others. On other occasions, we will see the appositeness of another. It is rather like a musical repertoire. Most of us know a few hymns (at least, a verse or two), several popular songs, and probably a couple of barroom ditties as well. Instinctively we choose to sing the songs more suitable to the circumstance and do not find it incongruous that the same song does not fit equally well into any situation. We learn to sing the music appropriate to the occasion so that, in any case, we can sing. Now, for the first time, we have a liturgical repertoire. As soon as we become familiar with the score, we should be able to celebrate in various situations with even more facility than in the past.

The common intention of the First and Second Services can easily be illustrated by the first two pages of each of the rites—pages which, except for the indications "First Service" and "Second Service", are identical. The first pages carries the title common to both:

## THE HOLY EUCHARIST
### The Liturgy for the Proclamation of The Word of God and Celebration of Holy Communion

*Prayer Book Studies XVII* made a good case for the selection in 1967 of the title: *The Liturgy of The Lord's Supper: The Celebration of Holy Eucharist and Ministration of Holy Communion*. When it came to selecting a title for the new materials, the Commission was forced to seek a new one for several reasons. First, these services were not simply the 1967 rite revised, and the Commission did not wish to create that impression by using the same title. Furthermore, the previous rite had an integrity of its own which deserved to be recognized by a distinctive title. And, finally, the 1967 rite had come to be known familiarly by its initials, as the LLS. (For the sake of convenience, we shall use the acronym LLS in future references throughout this book.)

Besides distinguishing the 1970 services from previous rites, the new title has a variety of advantages, the first of which is the simplicity of its primary heading: *The Holy Eucharist*. The word Eucharist is no longer strange to Episcopalians. Actually, the term is an ancient one, but its only use in the Prayer Book was in a rubric at the end of "An Office of Institution of Ministers"—scarcely a prominent position. In the past decade or so, however, the word has been used with increasing frequency. It has often been pointed out that the word is virtually a transliteration of the Greek and means thanksgiving. What we frequently fail to stress are the implications of using the word as a title. The term carries the weight of more than a formal, sincere expression of thanks. It means acting, thinking, *living* thankfully. It means man's recognition of himself as a creature, totally dependent upon God for his very being. It means man's awareness of himself as a sinner, redeemed solely by the gracious act of God. It means knowing that life is of God alone. And it means living in that recognition, awareness, and knowledge. Thus, to make Eucharist is not merely to engage in a formal act of worship, although it surely includes that; it is a style of life expressed in the term Eucharistic living—a style of life characteristic of the Body of Christ. Eucharist is not so much *what* we do as *how* we do it.

With the inclusion of "The Proclamation of The Word of God," the subtitle makes an emphasis that has been lacking in the titles of previous formularies. It is hardly necessary to make a case for the importance, indeed the necessity, of proclaiming the Word of God in the context of the liturgy. After all, such proclamation is the very *raison d'etre* for the existence of the church, and it has been a prominent part of our liturgical practice from the very beginning. Still, from time to time we Christians do tend to emphasize some one aspect of the truth at the expense of others. Furthermore, it is distressingly true that in our own time some churchmen have tended to posit a distinction between the proclamation of the Word of God and the celebration of the sacraments and then choose up sides. In fact, such distinctions are wholly arbitrary, as contemporary theologians are careful to point out. Orthodox scholar Alexander Schmemann states bluntly that "the proclamation of the word is a sacramental act *par excellence*." And the Dutch theologian Edward Schillebeeckx writes: "The proclamation cannot be separated from the liturgical Eucharistic action. . . . The whole Eucharistic celebration is one ministry of the word."

In the body of the First and Second Services the Commission seems to be perpetuating the fallacy that the two things can somehow be separated; one part of the service is labeled "The Proclamation of the Word of God" and another part "The Celebration of The Holy Communion." This is done, of course, merely as a matter of convenient reference. However, in view of the fact that most of us acquire what theology we know from our liturgical formularies, the choice of terminology seems rather unfortunate. Liturgical scholar H. Boone Porter, Jr., now Director of Roanridge, has what is surely the simplest answer to the dilemma; he is in the habit of referring to the two parts of the liturgy as "the first part of the service and the second part." This formula lends itself well to our present task and has therefore been gratefully adopted.

At any rate, we now have the Proclamation of The Word of God as a feature of the overall title and can rejoice in the official recognition of Proclamation as an essential part of our liturgical worship.

Celebration is another key word in the subtitle. Again, it is an ancient term that had fallen into disuse, probably as a result of our stubbornly Calvinist attitude toward worship. More recently, however, the term has been restored to the Christian's liturgical vocabulary. As it represents an important concept of liturgical worship, it deserves at least a brief examination.

The dictionary gives us the following definitions of the verb *to celebrate:*

1. To perform publicly and with appropriate rites. . . .
2. To honor or observe duly in some special way . . . especially by wholehearted or exuberant merrymaking.
3. To make known; proclaim; publish abroad.
4. To extol; to honor in a solemn manner; to sound the praises of . . .

A celebration is, of course, an act of celebrating.

Each of the above definitions finds its place and emphasis in the rites under consideration. Note the latter part of the second definition: "especially by wholehearted or exuberant merrymaking." Is not this the meaning we most often give to the word celebration? When we speak of an anniversary celebration, or a birthday celebration, or some sort of a victory celebration, or, for that matter, almost any time we speak of a celebration of any sort, do we not think first of a party where there will be "wholehearted merrymaking"?

A celebration is something we eagerly look forward to, prepare for, and, if the event to be celebrated is of importance to us, join in wholeheartedly and exuberantly. It is normally a joyous occasion. Such a celebration may, of course, take many different forms; it may include the parade, watermelon feast, and fireworks of a Fourth of July; it may be a quiet candlelight supper between two lovers on their tenth wedding anniversary; it may be ice cream and cake, paper hats and games on a sixth birthday; it may include a gold watch and a steak dinner after fifty years with the company; it may be a snake dance after winning the homecoming game.

Whatever form it may take, this is the sort of thing most of us have in mind when we think of a celebration. It is a joyous occasion, accompanied by appropriate rites and ceremonies, entered into wholeheartedly, even exuberantly.

This aspect of a celebration is not lost in the proposed rites; indeed, it is given increased emphasis and dignity. All the way through both services the tone is one of a joyous occasion into which the participants enter wholeheartedly and exuberantly. The word exuberant may sound a bit exaggerated to some Episcopalians. If the term bothers you, substitute the word enthusiastically. To be enthusiastic means to be filled with the Holy Spirit. You will find that the trial-use rites intend to provide a vehicle for genuine enthusiasm.

This is not, of course, the only aspect of celebration as defined by the dictionary; nor are the other elements of the definition overlooked in the new formularies. The very fact that they are liturgical rites fulfills the first and second parts of the definition: "To honor or observe duly in some special way . . . to perform publicly and with appropriate rites."

The third definition, "To make known; proclaim; publish abroad," ties in with our previous discussion and receives its first emphasis in the title itself. Later, in place after place, we will discover the intention of the services to fulfill this definition—not just explicitly in the words, but implicitly in the whole liturgical action.

Finally, one of the chief functions of the liturgy is to "extol; to honor in a solemn manner; to sound the praises of. . . ." The One whom we extol in the liturgy, honor solemnly, sound the praises of, is none other than the one true God: Father, Son, and Holy Spirit. We do not, in the eucharistic liturgy, celebrate just any joyful occasion that may occur to us. Rather, we celebrate the most important thing we know: salvation—the gracious act of God in granting us life in Christ through the work of the Holy Spirit. There can be no more significant cause for celebration than this. Note that we do not merely commemorate, we *celebrate!* (Incidentally, the word "solemn" does not mean somber or gloomy, but, to quote the dictionary once more, "with religious sanction . . . with full liturgical ceremony.")

Thus, the character of the liturgy is that of a true celebration: seeking to extol, honor, and proclaim God's mighty acts for the salvation of mankind by public observance with appropriate rites, entered into wholeheartedly and exuberantly. The new rites make it more clear than ever before that the entire worshipping body is a part of the celebration. As we become more and more aware of the celebrative aspect of our worship, we may find our manner of speaking changing. Perhaps we shall no longer find it appropriate to speak of "attending Mass" or "making our Communion" but of "celebrating the Eucharist." In the past, this term has unfortunately been reserved primarily for the priest. We say: "Father Jones celebrated this morning." Of course, this is true; but it is only part of the truth. If I was present, I, too, celebrated, although I may not be in priest's orders. One who participates in a celebration is a celebrant. Every participant in the liturgy is a celebrant. It may be that we will learn to say: "We celebrated the Eucharist this morning with Father Jones."

All of these concepts—Eucharist, Proclamation, Celebration—are tied together by referring to them as The Liturgy. Since the word liturgy has been restored to popular use in recent years, its etymology and development have been rehearsed repeatedly. In spite of its interesting history, the thing that most concerns us is the way we use the term today. There seem to be three important elements in our modern definition of liturgy. First, it refers to a form of worship and is thereby distinguished from all other rituals that we engage in more or less frequently. It is corporate in nature; that is, liturgy is an expression of, and action by, the Body of Christ of which all Christians are members. As such, it is to be distinguished from crowd or mass action. Furthermore, it is *deliberately* corporate, as opposed to accidentally. This does not mean that a liturgy may not allow for a spontaneous expression, but, as Clarence Rivers points out: "Spontaneity takes a great deal of practice." This leads to the third element in a definition of liturgy: by common usage it is normally restricted to worship that is relatively structured. In summary, then, we can define liturgy as it is popularly used today as a structured, corporate expression of worship.

So, all the important words of our title convey concepts that modify and expand one another. We worship God *by means of* a liturgy; the *content* of the liturgy is Proclamation; the *form* of the liturgy is Communion, the sacred meal; its *nature* is Eucharistic; and its *character* is that of a Celebration.

The back of the title page is at least as notable as the title itself and, in practice, undoubtedly will be the object of more attention. The most prominent feature is the heading: "Concerning the Celebration." In the text that follows, no attempt is made to define or defend celebration. The word is left to carry its own meaning; and we recall the elements of the dictionary definition: honor, special, proclaim, extol, whole-hearted, exuberant. The concept is not argued, it is assumed. Even more, it is lifted up and given a primary emphasis. The lack of any explanation, the confident, almost casual, reference to the liturgy as a celebration, is surely the most significant thing about the use of the term here. Almost everyone has a functional definition of a celebration even if he has not looked it up in the dictionary. That is, he knows one when he sees one. Well, that is what the liturgy is intended to be! No apology needed.

As we move beyond the heading into the text itself, we are met in the very first sentence by a remarkable statement: "The Holy Eucharist is the principal act of Christian worship on the Lord's Day." The statement is not remarkable because of *what* it says, but because it *is* said. Few Episcopalians, if any, would disagree with the content of the sentence—*in theory*. In actual practice, there are many parishes where the theory is stretched almost beyond recognition when "the principal act of Christian worship" is done by a handful of early risers at a side altar while the main body of Christians will gather at a later hour to do something other than celebrate the Holy Eucharist. There is a variety of reasons—historical, political, and even accidental—why this practice has become the custom of some congregations, most of whom have long since given up trying to formulate a theological justification for it.

Why, then, bother to make such a statement at all, much less in such a conspicuous spot? Certainly it is true, but virtually everyone already agrees that it is true, at least in theory. Moreover, among some Episcopalians, acknowledgment of that truth is not seen as sufficient reason to alter a long-standing practice. The occurrence here of this statement is not likely to persuade anyone to change, nor does it appear to be designed to do so. Instead, this is evidently a case of "making a statement for the record." Although the truth has long been acknowledged, there has been no explicit statement to that effect in any of our official formularies. The absence of such a formulation has been used on occasion as an "argument from silence." Apparently the Standing Liturgical Commission feels that it is about time we gave official expression to this important concept. This has been done in as clear, concise, and unargumentative a way as possible, and in the most appropriate place, as if to say: "Before we talk about celebrating the Holy Eucharist, let us remind ourselves that we are talking about the principal act of Christian worship on the Lord's Day."

Then follows a series of statements that appeared first in the LLS under the heading: "The Ministers of the Liturgy." These simply set forth the liturgical roles appropriate to the various orders of ministry: lay persons, deacons, priests, and bishops. The intent here is not to set restrictions on laymen and deacons. On the contrary, it is to remind us that each of the orders has a traditional role in the liturgical action and to encourage the recognition and exercise of these roles.

The final paragraph in these prefatory notes (excluding the brief reference noting where additional suggestions may be found) authorizes the use of Morning or Evening Prayer as the first part of the liturgy. The reason for this (which *PBS 21* assures us is "in response to many requests") was not to provide more flexibility in the eucharistic liturgy nor because the rites do not in themselves incorporate all the features found in the Offices. It was, rather, an almost opposite consideration that led to this provision. In the preparation of the LLS, the first part of the service was deliberately designed so that, by exercising certain options, it might be used *in place of* Morning Prayer in those parishes where tradition dictated something other than the Eucharist at the main services several weeks of the month. It was hoped that the use of the first part of the LLS in place of the Office would satisfy the "Morning Prayer people" while at the same time gradually introducing them to the advantages of a full celebration each week. The plan failed. Those who delight in the Sunday morning choral version of Morning Prayer were not to be denied.

But an unexpected development appeared. A good many parishes began to experiment with a sort of "optional rider." An announcement would be printed in the service sheet, or made at the time other announcements were given, that immediately following Morning Prayer, allowing only for a brief time lapse, the Liturgy of the Lord's Supper would be celebrated, beginning with the Offering of the elements. Anyone should feel free to leave as usual at the conclusion of the Office; on the other hand, all communicants were invited to remain for the celebration. Reports from these several parishes indicate a surprising and gratifying response. The new paragraph was drawn with the intention of regularizing such experiments and encouraging other congregations in a similar direction if they feel it would be desirable and helpful.

Even a quick first reading of this page of general directions makes it quite clear that we will be dealing here with a new style of formulary. We are met in every paragraph with words such as appropriate and fitting, should and may. This is a far cry from the restrictive, how-to-do-it rubrics of the past. There is no hint here of legalism, no attempt to set forth a comprehensive list of rules and regulations. What we find instead is the statement of some general principles, guidelines rather than laws. As such, they deserve to be taken seriously, perhaps even more seriously than a dogmatic statement of law. A rule is, after all, only a rule; it is either adhered to or broken and one is usually quite clear about which course he has followed. A guiding principle, on the other hand, demands another sort of commitment and may, on different occasions, result in quite different sets of actions.

As we proceed to examine the rites, it will become increasingly apparent that that is the general tenor of the rubrics throughout. In the interest of preserving an essential basic structure, some rubrics unequivocally direct certain things to be said or done at particular points. But by far the majority follow the style of those on the opening page, setting the tone for the whole range of rubrical instructions. Undoubtedly, some will view this practice as a tendency toward laxness; actually, it has to do with responsibility. It is a recognition that ultimate responsibility for the liturgical celebration (within certain basic principles) belongs to the local worshipping community. The concept of liturgical uniformity has always existed more as a myth than as actual practice anyway. Now, the responsibility is clearly recognized as belonging where it has, in fact, always rested.

It is almost as though the drafting committee had deliberately taken as its guiding rule a statement by the English scholar G. D. Kilpatrick: "There must be controls but they must be limited and subordinate. Priest and people must enjoy the freedom to go forward until they are told to stop. We do not want a reign of legality which insists that they stop until they are told to go forward." It is precisely that philosophy that informs the rubrical directions in the new rites.

Furthermore, it is important to emphasize that *both* the First and the Second Service share the opening set of guidelines and the general tone of rubrical direction set there. As a result, the First Service (basically the 1928 rite rearranged) has possibilities for local adaptation never before open to those congregations who prefer the more traditional formularies. A whole new pattern of freedom that can lead to increased delight in our worship has been established. With freedom, of course, comes the responsibility for an even deeper understanding of, and commitment to, liturgical worship.

As in the earlier LLS, the opening of the service is not given a title. This probably reflects no more than the fact that the several subheadings under each of the major divisions are given primarily as a matter of convenient reference. That being the case, the beginning of the service obviously requires no special designation.

Since 1967 this portion of the service has been increasingly referred to as the Entrance. That is due in part to a phrase in the opening rubric, and in part to ancient usage. Normally, it would be as good a shorthand designation as any; however, as we shall see, it just might not be actually descriptive of the purpose of this section of the liturgy.

In terms of the structure alone, the opening provides more flexibility than any other part of the rite.

The various components of the opening are generally common to all the trial use rites, but their arrangement and provisions for optional use allow for a wide variation in the ordering of any one rite as well as between the rites.

That variety is graphically illustrated by the following chart showing the several elements and options within each of the trial use rites. Material that is invariable is printed in all capital letters; options are indicated by the use of parentheses.

| *LLS (1967)* | *First Service* | *Second Service* |
| --- | --- | --- |
| (Penitential Order) | (Penitential Order) | (Penitential Order) |
| (Song) | (Song) | (Song) |
| GREETING | (Opening Sentence) | GREETING |
| (Peace) | | |
| COLLECT FOR PURITY | COLLECT FOR PURITY | (Collect For Purity) |
| SUMMARY OF LAW | SUMMARY OF LAW (or Decalogue or both) | |
| LORD, HAVE MERCY [1] (or Glory Be to God or Te Deum) | LORD, HAVE MERCY [1] (May be omitted if Decalogue is said) (Glory Be to God[2]) [3] | GLORY TO GOD IN THE HIGHEST [2] (or, Lord, have mercy[1]) [3] |

[1] May use any of several versions.

[2] Or some other hymn of praise. Appointed for use Christmas through Epiphany, Sundays in Easter; optional at other times, but not to be used during Advent or Lent except on weekday feasts.

[3] In the First and Second Services, the Litany, concluding with the Kyries, may replace the entire Entrance rite above.

The First Service is obviously the most traditional. There are two principal differences between this arrangement and that of the 1928 Prayer Book. The first is that one of the Opening Sentences from

Morning Prayer may be used to precede the opening Collect, commonly called the Collect For Purity. The provision merely regularizes a practice that is already a familiar one in many congregations. For some years now, clergy and people have felt that the 1928 service opened somewhat abruptly. On Sunday morning, the usual practice was to have an opening hymn during the entrance of the ministers. In any event, everyone would be standing. Then, suddenly and with no prelude at all, the priest would begin the Collect. Normally, the first line or two of the prayer would be missed amid the confusion and noise of everyone's kneeling. Some clergy resorted to using the salutation "The Lord be with you" and its familiar response. This worked very well mechanically but somehow still seemed abrupt and, in addition, the formula is in danger of being drastically overworked. The use of one of the sentences from Morning Prayer has the two-fold advantage of beginning the service with a proper greeting and also of striking the appropriate seasonal or thematic note. Thus, the liturgy begins smoothly and on the up-beat.

The other change from 1928 is the transference of the hymn "Glory be to God on high" from the end of the service to its more traditional and esthetically proper place in the beginning. This had been previously done in 1967 and confirms the experience of many congregations who have been using it in this place for years.

The Ten Commandments are not printed in the text of the rite because of their infrequent use. However, the full Decalogue, with responses, is appended to the service and reference is made to the page number where it may be easily located when desired.

Thus, the First Service allows an opening that is virtually identical, in both words and structure, to that with which any Episcopalian will be familiar. At the same time, it provides the possibility of some interesting variations. For instance, either the First or Second Service may be begun with the Litany. In this case, the Litany may conclude with "Lord, have mercy" and may completely displace all of the opening part of the rite. It would be entirely fitting to begin the liturgy in one of the penitential seasons (Advent or Lent) with the singing of the Litany in procession, rather than with the customary processional hymn. Then, the celebration would continue with the next section, *i.e.*, the Salutation and the Collect of the Day. Or, a Penitential Order may be used in place of the Greeting and Collect For Purity.

The term Entrance, then, might not be an adequate description of an opening that could very well serve the purpose of preparing the congregation to participate in the liturgy.

By way of contrast to the First Service, the opening of the Second allows for considerable streamlining. It may be as brief as a Greeting, followed by a form of "Lord, have mercy"; or it may be elaborated to include a psalm, a prayer, and a song of praise.

The key is adaptability. By the judicious exercise of the options provided, the celebration can be opened on a note entirely appropriate to virtually any occasion or context.[1] It may be elaborate and rich—almost a liturgy within a liturgy—or it may be brief and to the point. In either event, it can set the tone for all that is to follow as it is obviously dependent upon what is to come and points eagerly beyond itself. The People of God are assembled in the Name of the Lord, made aware of the purpose of their gathering, and are ready to commence the celebration!

The familiar salutation, response, and invitation to prayer form the transition from the opening part of the service to the first major subdivision, entitled: THE PROCLAMATION OF THE WORD OF GOD. At this point all the trial-use rites follow the same traditional structure: Collect, Scripture Lesson, Gospel Reading, Sermon and Creed. The new materials provide us with opportunities for the enrichment of our liturgy at several points.

The first is in the matter of the selections for Lessons. In addition to a portion of the Gospel— which is at the very heart of our life as a Church and, therefore, indispensible to our celebration of that life —one or two other portions of Scripture may be read. There may, for instance, be a reading from the Old Testament in addition to, or in place of, a reading from the Epistles or other writings of the New Testament. An Old Testament reading was first provided for in 1967; then, in 1969, provision was made for

---

[1] It is interesting to see that the theme of celebration is already struck in the Collect For Purity; note the phrase: "worthily magnify thy holy Name" and compare the fourth definition of *to celebrate* on page 30.

this to replace a reading from the Epistles if desired. The reason for this is that many congregations feel a deep need for hearing Lessons which were the very foundation of Israel, out of which Christianity was formed. The New Israel is the successor to the Old. The New Covenant fulfills the Old and makes it new. It is most appropriate, then, that we should constantly be reminded of our inheritance in and through the great Old Testament passages read in the context of the Christian Eucharist. But the older rites already prescribed readings from the Epistles as well as from the Gospels, and three Lessons seemed just a bit much for most people—especially as they frequently were chosen without sufficient regard for the relationship between the various portions.

Now, we have the option of using either the Old Testament, or some writings of the New Testament, or a combination of both. Furthermore, another volume in the series of trial-use materials (*Prayer Book Studies 19*) provides us with a variety of selections from Old Testament, Epistles, and Gospels for each Sunday and Holy Day of the Christian year. The great benefit of the expanded list of readings probably will not be apparent to the average Churchman in terms of the variety itself. After all, most of us do not remember what Epistle or Gospel selection we heard on the Third Sunday After Easter last year. Even if we did, these lessons probably make up most, if not all, the Bible reading we normally experience, and we could very well stand to hear the same scripture read a year apart. Where most Churchmen will notice the difference, hopefully, is in the preaching that follows.

Many clergy seem to feel that by the time they have preached four or five sermons on the same set of proper lessons, they have just about exhausted their understanding of that portion of Scripture. Then, they are apt to resort either to preaching on some subject other than the appointed readings or, worse yet, attempt to rehash some old sermon. Whether they are justified in this feeling is not the question; it has happened with alarming frequency, and the new arrangement is designed to alleviate the situation. Surely, no preacher will now lack for sufficient and relevant Scriptural resources for a lifetime of preaching.

In *The Book of Common Prayer* the Collect, Epistle, and Gospel are printed out in full. Two factors militate against the continuance of this practice, at least as concerns the Scripture portions. One is the expanded list of selections, providing, on the average, three possibilities from each, the Old Testament, the Epistles, and the Gospels. Secondly, so many versions of the Bible are now authorized for use in church that it would be virtually impossible to provide each selection in every authorized version.

That should prove to be a blessing. Very few portions of the Bible, if any, were written to be read with the eye; they were written to be proclaimed aloud and heard with the ear. Even the Letters of St Paul and the other New Testament writers were intended, at least for the most part, to be read aloud to the assembled community. That is why they are read aloud in churches today. Their impact is still greatest when they are heard. After all, most of our congregations today are literate. If it were simply a matter of imparting information, or if it were true that they could gain more benefit by reading the Scripture than by hearing it proclaimed, it would be much more efficient to announce a few moments of silence while everyone turned to page whatever and read to himself the Gospel appointed for the day.

There is, of course, a place for private, individual Bible reading, just as there is for private prayer. But just as corporate prayer of the liturgy serves a different function from private prayer, even so the public proclamation of the Word serves an entirely different function from private reading for either devotions or study: it is a public, corporate liturgical *act,* involving the worshipping Body as a whole. At this point in the liturgy, our participant role calls for hearing.

For the proclamation of the Word to be effective, at least two things are required: good, audible, intelligent reading and attentive listening. Perhaps it is the scarcity of these two vital elements that has led many to resort to reading the lessons for themselves even while they were being read aloud. With the lessons not so convenient for the congregation, it just may be—at least it can be hoped for—that both reading and listening habits will be forced to improve.

Recently, Episcopalians have begun to feel and experience a great deal more freedom with regard to their posture during the service. Many of us were nurtured on the dictum: "Kneel to pray, stand to praise, sit for instruction." Of course, that was never an invariable rule, and we broke it often; for instance, we were taught to stand for the prayers during

Baptism, Holy Matrimony, and at other times. We sit to hear the New Testament read during the Daily Office, but when the very same selection is appointed as the Gospel for the Eucharist, we stand. So, the familiar little slogan was always more of a catch phrase than a rule. Pragmatically, many Churchmen adopted a more reliable guide to posture: "do whatever the choir does" and "don't commit yourself until you see what those around you are going to do." That saved us from the embarrassment of being conspicuous by standing up while everyone else was kneeling.

Lately, however, we are discovering the benefits of trying out other postures than those to which we have been accustomed. This is one of the reasons why there are only a minimum number of directions in the new rites about standing, sitting, or kneeling. There is something to be said for the corporate worshipping body acting in unison—at least much of the time—as an indication that the doing of the liturgy is a corporate act rather than a gathering of individuals, each doing his own thing. However, many of the decisions about corporate action are better made in the worshipping community itself. By leaving such ceremonial practices to the determination of the local congregation, these rites make it possible to adapt the new services to our current habits while at the same time freeing us to experiment with different and perhaps more meaningful practices.

On the other hand, certain postures are so obviously appropriate at certain points that it seems well to indicate them in the rubrics. That is why we are bidden to be seated during the reading of the Lessons. Then, to accord the honor customarily and rightly due to the Gospel, we are directed to stand while hearing it proclaimed. (Apparently it seemed superfluous to add that the congregation may sit to hear the sermon.)

At this point we should note one of the directions included under the heading "Concerning the Celebration": "Lay persons appointed by the presiding Minister should normally be assigned the reading of the Lessons which precede the Gospel." This instruction is just as significant for what it does *not* say as for what it *does*. It *does* say, quite definitely, that the reading of the Old Testament and the Epistle is a part of the liturgy that legitimately belongs to the laity. It is part of the layman's liturgy. For it to be taken from him by clerical fiat is unthinkable; for him to relinquish it is for him to neglect his obligation as well as his privilege. The direction does *not* specify that the lay person be male. The only requirement should be a good reading voice, clearly audible. Many women can meet that requirement, sometimes better than men. Furthermore, there in no mention of vestments. There is no reason why the reader, male or female, cannot rise from his regular place in the congregation at the appointed time, proceed to a place from which he can be seen and heard clearly, read the assigned Lesson, then return to his place. On the other hand, there is nothing to prevent the reader from being vested in cassock and surplice, academic gown, or any suitable habit, and seated in the choir or with the other Ministers. The important thing is not where the reader sits, or what he or she wears, but the fact that a lay person performs a liturgical role.

Following each of the Lessons there may be a psalm, hymn, or anthem. Again, we are given an opportunity for the enrichment of our worship by the use of our most ancient hymnal, the Psalter. In fact, it should be pointed out that a psalm may be used wherever there is an optional selection of music. It may be too much to expect that many of our congregations will return to the practice of singing the psalms—the way the Psalter was intended to be used, and indeed was used up until just two or three generations ago. However, now that some new, easy-to-sing settings for congregational use are readily available, perhaps a few of us will have such an opportunity. In addition, the Standing Liturgical Commission is preparing a new and interesting version of the Psalter for liturgical use. At the time of this writing, *Prayer Book Studies 23* has been published, containing 71 of the most frequently-used of the 150 psalms, and work is proceeding on revision of the remainder. The new material may be further inducement to many of our congregations to employ the Psalter as a regular feature of their eucharistic worship.

Immediately following the reading of the Gospel comes the sermon. Logically and dramatically, this is the proper sequence: first the proclamation of the Word; then the exposition of the Word; the Word read, the Word expounded. Later, at the altar, Christ, the Word made flesh, will be broken and distributed. Now, the Word of God in the Scriptures is broken and distributed. The first recorded sermon of our Lord followed this pattern: "He went to the synagogue, as his custom was, on the sabbath day. And he stood up to read . . . . And he closed the book . . . and the eyes of all in the synagogue were fixed on him. And he began to say them . . ." (*Luke 4:16 ff.*, *RSV*)

The natural sequence is to read, then to expound. The dramatic effect is obvious: without any intervening words or actions to detract or take one's mind from the portion of Scripture, the preacher plunges immediately into the sermon. Sometimes, alas, the connection between Scripture and Sermon is somewhat remote, to say the least (perhaps "subtle" would be a more charitable description). At any rate, whatever connection there is—and *surely* there will be some—it should be a bit more obvious in this sort of juxtaposition than in an arrangement in which five to seven minutes, filled with Creed, announcements, and hymn, have lapsed between the reading and the preaching. The arrangement was first provided for in the LLS. However, in response to irresistible pressures from the clergy, a provision was made in 1969 that "a psalm or hymn may be said or sung before or after the sermon." That concession is retained in the 1970 rites. Because the permissive rubric is relegated to the back and not printed within the text proper, we can hope that it will frequently be overlooked—at least insofar as it causes an interruption between the reading and the preaching of the Word. The new structure, coupled with the expanded selection of readings, should have a salutary effect upon liturgical preaching.

Following the proclamation and exposition of the Gospel, it is put into context by our recitation of the Nicene Creed. It is impractical, obviously, to read the entire Gospel narrative at any one service. Likewise, it is impossible to preach the whole of the Gospel story in any one sermon (although one occasionally hears a neophyte preacher make an attempt to do so). Instead, the Lessons and the sermon concentrate upon only one episode or facet of what is in reality an inseparable whole. Therefore, it is good for us to be reminded of this necessary selectivity by having the Lesson and sermon placed in perspective. The Creed is, in effect, the whole Gospel in outline form.

The Creed is a liturgical symbol. It is not intended to be a comprehensive theological statement. Like the Bible itself, it is subject to theological interpretation, and entire theological libraries have been written about it. Furthermore, as a liturgical formula, it is necessarily corporate in nature. That is, like our hymns, our prayers, our confessions and our thanksgivings, it is an expression of the total body rather than of individuals. It is, after all, a statement of faith; faith belongs to the Church, not to the individuals. As individuals we subscribe to the creedal affirmations of the Church, but we can do so only as members of the Body of Christ. The Creed is what the Church believes. As individual members, each of us shares that common belief; but it is a belief that we hold *in common*. We participate in the belief of the Church in much the same sense that we participate in the liturgy, the sacraments, the eternal life of the Body of Christ: not merely as the sum total of a collection of individuals, but as members of the one corporate Body. Our identification is in the Body, not apart from it.

Provision is made to omit the Creed on most weekdays, but on Sundays and other festivals, when it is expected that the whole worshipping body will be gathered, the Creed is used: 1) to set the Proclamation in its proper context; 2) as an expression of our corporate faith; and 3) as a symbol of the unity of Christ's Body, the Creed being one of the symbols acceptable to, and used by, virtually all traditions of Christianity.

The ecumenical dimension has led to the recommendation that a new traslation of the Creed be used at all celebrations of the Eucharist. The new version is one drawn up by the International Commission on English Texts (ICET), a group composed of representatives of the Roman Catholic Church, Anglicans, and virtually all the mainstream traditions of Protestant Christianity from all over the English-speaking world. Thus, the commission is both international and ecumenical. *PBS 21* includes a detailed account of the history of the ICET and its work. For our purposes, we need note only a couple of points. The ICET itself is not an authoritative body. It is a work/study group organized to do basic research and to propose to the several churches liturgical formulae which it would seem that each of those bodies could accept.

The purpose is fairly obvious. Virtually all eucharistic liturgies incorporate certain common texts such as the Creed, the Lord's Prayer, "Glory be to God on high," "Lift up your hearts," "Holy, Holy, Holy," etc. Through the centuries, mostly by accident and by virtue of independent translations from Greek and Latin texts, the several traditions have found themselves using somewhat variant forms of the same symbols. That seems to be an unnecessary aspect of denominationalism. If we could discover forms for these great Christian symbols that we could all agree to use, we could more obviously and more consciously proclaim and celebrate the essential unity of the Body of Christ.

We are being asked to use the new versions on an experimental basis. The only instance of the work of the ICET in the First Service is the Nicene Creed. In the Second Service, we find ICET recommended texts being used in a number of places. Except for the Creed, the new texts lend themselves more readily to rites employing the contemporary idiom, and so they are not suggested for use in the more traditional First Service.

It should be stated as clearly as possible that the ICET does *not* intend to be writing a *new* Creed. Nor does the Standing Liturgical Commission, in recommending this version, believe that a new Creed is being proposed. The new version is an attempt to preserve the historical statement common to virtually all of Christianity; to clarify some of the more trouble-some obscurities and ambiguities; and at the same time to do all that in words that will be acceptable to all the several traditions of the Church. That is a pretty tall order. Whether or not the present version will fulfill those goals is yet to be seen. However, the ICET texts have been accepted for experimental use by a number of the participant bodies and there is considerable sentiment—and hope—for eventual success.

The three elements that follow the Creed are common to all the trial-use rites: Prayers of Intercession, Confession and Absolution, and the exchange of the Peace. As we shall see, a great deal of variety is provided in the words used for each of these as well as in the manner of their performance. But the first thing to be noted about them is the options allowed for the order in which they occur. It has already been mentioned that the penitential material may be used as a separate service, or preceding the liturgy itself, and we will explore that possibility in greater detail. Still, the most common use of these three elements undoubtedly will be at the point where they are printed in the texts of the rites.

In the LLS, the Penitential Order was printed in an appendix, but the heading appeared at this place in the service, followed by the Peace and the Prayers. In the text of the First Service, the Prayers appear first, then the Confession and Absolution are printed in full, followed by the Peace. The Peace is again the last to appear in the Second Service, but the order of the other two items is reversed: Confession, then Prayers. The three rites may be compared in the following table:

| *LLS (1967)* | *First Service* | *Second Service* |
| --- | --- | --- |
| Penitential Order | Prayers | Penitential Order |
| Peace | Penitential Order | Prayers |
| Prayers | Peace | Peace |

Rubrics then provide that the LLS may be arranged in the same order as the Second Service, but not that of the First. However, the order of the First and Second Services may follow *any of the three sequences* shown above. The only limitation on the arrangement of these elements is the direction that the exchange of the Peace should not precede the Confession and Absolution.

The advantage of this flexibility is that any congregation using the new materials may, if desired, follow exactly the same sequence no matter which of the new rites they are doing. If, on the other hand, it seems better to do so, they may use a somewhat different order of things for each of the rites. The order of printing in the First and Second Services is not intended to indicate preference. The order of the First Service was chosen because it follows the order that occurs in the Prayer Book (with the addition of the Peace) and every attempt was made to keep the First Service as near to the 1928 form as possible. That order was deliberately reversed in the Second Service not only to demonstrate the possibility of another sequence but also to illustrate some of the advantages (and perhaps disadvantages) of choosing it as an option.

For two reasons, we shall examine each of these components in the order in which they are printed in the Second Service. First, we are already accustomed to the sequence as it appears in the First Service, and it seems to require no particular explanation. In addition, the sequence printed in the Second Service is an arrangement possible to both the LLS and to the First Service.

Before doing so, however, we should emphasize again the desirability of experimenting with all the possible arrangements, including omissions and additions as allowed. That is the obvious advantage of trial use. Too frequently, that advantage has been allowed to go unclaimed. Reading the text of a rite simply does not give one the experience of participation in the liturgy. It is impossible to predetermine the reaction of any given congregation to a new liturgical practice—it must be tried, not once only, but a sufficient number of times for the strangeness to wear off. Then, and not until then, can a responsible judgment be attempted. Until we have actually experienced each of the possible variations, we will never know what delights we may have been missing.

In 1967 the Liturgical Commission thought that by printing the Penitential Order in an appendix they would be making it more convenient for everyone. If it were to be used in one of the allowable positions other than where the heading was printed, it would be easy to locate and its appearance in one particular place would not impede the flow of the service when it was used elsewhere or omitted. However, what was intended as a convenience was viewed by many Churchmen as a sneaky attempt to do away with corporate confession altogether. Actually, the rubrics themselves should have obviated any such concern: *PBS XVII* provided a clear rationale for the arrangement, and *Introduction to The Liturgy of The Lord's Supper* stated unequivocally that the Penitential Order *may be used* at *all* celebrations and that it need not ever be omitted.

Even so, it became necessary to publish in the "Schedule Of Variations" in 1969 the statement: "The Penitential Order is a normal part of the service, but it may be omitted on appropriate occasions." Originally, five distinctly *in*appropriate occasions were specified. Now, the definition of an appropriate occasion is left up to the worshipping congregation and, theoretically, they might omit the penitential material invariably. However, the new rubric appears to have satisfied those who feared that the Commission was trying to do away with the liturgical confession and absolution of sin. Printing a form of confession at some point in the text of the rite should further satisfy those who were made uncomfortable by the previous arrangement. The 1969 rubric is included, and there should no longer be any doubt that some form of penitential material, used in one place or another, is the intended norm.

As printed in the First Service, the penitential material is virtually identical with that in the 1928

Prayer Book. With the exception of one or two minor verbal changes, the Invitation, Confession, and Absolution are the familiar texts. The only really noticeable change is in the Comfortable Words. In the first place, their use has been made optional. That was done primarily for the benefit of those who, especially on weekdays, would appreciate possibilities for shortening the service without sacrificing any essential elements. When the Words are used, they are placed before the Absolution rather than after it, following an arrangement first proposed in 1967 and one which has met with general approval. Finally, the ascription of authorship has been omitted. Only the first was spoken by our Lord, so the original introduction was misleading; but the important fact is not who wrote them but that they comprise "the Word of God to all who truly turn to him."

In the First Service we find an alternative form of confession printed right in the text. Many will see the new form as a welcome improvement over the extreme subjectivity and verbosity of the older one. It says the same thing, but in a more direct, matter-of-fact way. There is yet another alternative provided for in the First Service. In an appendix we find a complete Penitential Order, and a third form of confession is printed there, along with the alternative just mentioned. Thus, we have a choice of three possible forms in the First Service.

Surprisingly enough, the Second Service shows less flexibility at this point than does the First. There is only one form of Confession printed in the text, and it is the same one that appears in the appended

Penitential Order. It doesn't appear likely that there would be any official objection to the use in the Second Order of any of the Penitential materials provided for the First. However, the question is not likely to arise. The form that appears was written specifically for the Second Service and is so in keeping with the language, style, and tone of the service that it no doubt will be considered thoroughly suitable at whatever point it is used when a confession is appointed. The Comfortable Words are omitted entirely from the Second Service, and a different form of the Absolution is provided.

A word should be added about the Penitential Order in the Appendix. Many congregations found it was helpful, on occasions or regularly, to place the penitential material before the liturgy. Provision for that was made in the LLS, and one example of how it was used is as follows. At the scheduled hour of the service, the ministers, vested in albs, amices, and stoles, stood at the steps of the chancel and led the congregation in a service of preparation; *i.e.,* the Penitential Order. Then the ministers returned to the sacristy to vest in chasubles and, perhaps after a brief interval of silent meditation, the eucharistic celebration began with the usual procession. Still other congregations found the Penitential Order useful as a separate service entirely. In order to do that successfully, however, they were forced to improvise a great deal.

Therefore, the Penitential Order has now been expanded to provide a complete service in itself which may be used before the liturgy or at other times.

Provision has been made for the inclusion of such elements as a sermon, prayers, and concluding grace. If the experience of the last three years is indicative, this new service should find a place in the devotional practices of many parishes.

Finally, it should be noted that "on appropriate occasions" the penitential material may be omitted altogether. Whenever that is done, we are specifically directed to include a penitential petition in the Prayers. Furthermore, we should not overlook the fact that the greatest of all petitions for forgiveness is contained within the Lord's Prayer which comes at the conclusion of the consecration. And what further absolution could man desire than to receive into his hands and his mouth the very Body and Blood of our Lord. The whole sacramental action is based upon the forgiving act of God in Christ, of which the communion itself is the symbol *par excellence*.

It is at the point of the corporate prayers of the congregation that the greatest need has been felt for flexibility and variety. And it is precisely at this point that we find the richest possibilities for adaptation to the needs of the local community.

The First Service provides us with a slightly revised version of the familiar "Prayer For the Whole State of Christ's Church." There are a few verbal changes, especially at the beginning and the end, and a petition has been added that we might be good stewards of all God's creation. Even so, it is immediately recognizable as "Prayer Book."

However, the rubrics direct our attention to an

appendix where we find seven additional Forms of Intercession provided. And most of these allow for considerable flexibility by additions and omissions. The several forms vary in length and in structure, but they all include a common basic body of content. Nonetheless, each of the suggested forms has its own flavor and its own unique contributions. Two are written in litany style, two in the style of a "responsive reading." One is primarily a bidding prayer, one is a series of short prayers or collects, and one is chiefly an outline to be filled in by prayers of the congregation.

Several of the forms are designed so that they can simply be read by the minister appointed if necessary. However, all of them invite and encourage some degree of verbal participation by the entire congregation—which might range all the way from a repeated, litany-like phrase ("Lord, have mercy") to the composition and offering of virtually the entire prayer. Even the traditional form printed in the text of the First Service provides for congregational responses following each of the petitions.

In the Second Service, none of the prayers is actually printed in the text; there is only the basic outline and a reference to the appendix where various Forms of Intercession may be found. The rubric in the Second Service seems to be one of those deliberate Anglican ambiguities. That is, it is obviously intended that one of the Forms provided should normally be used. In view of the variety offered, and the fact that several of them are "wide open," the material provided undoubtedly will prove adequate to virtually any occasion. On the other hand, no drafting committee can possibly foresee every eventuality, and no set of texts could be expected to meet every unusual need. Under extraordinary circumstances, it would not appear to be in violation of the spirit (or the words) of the rubric to compose an entirely original prayer or series of prayers—provided only that such follow the skeletal outline provided.

At this vital point in the liturgy, the rite may be—and should be—custom-tailored to fit the individual worshipping community. Furthermore, the community is different each time it meets, and that is true even if its membership should remain exactly constant. A week later (even a day later) every member of that community will be a different person in many ways, and the total body will be relatively even more changed. Thus, the concerns and the prayers vary not only between congregations, but from time to time within the same community. The Forms of Intercession are designed to speak to and for the body of worshippers gathered—a particular body, at a specific place, in a discreet moment of time.

Much of the liturgy—most of it—serves precisely the opposite function. That is, it deliberately seeks to place the individual congregation in the larger context of the whole Body of Christ and the cosmos, with the angels and archangels and the whole company of heaven. Furthermore, it functions to establish the unity of time—past, present, and future. Spatial and temporal integrity is one of the chief emphases of the liturgy, and the maintenance of that integrity is one of the most important things a liturgy is supposed to do. But if Christianity is to avoid the trap of living in the past on the one hand, or, on the other, of existing in a sort of suspended animation while waiting for the "pie in the sky bye-and-bye," there must be an urgent sense of the *now*. Likewise, if such concepts as the brotherhood of man and love of neighbor are to be translated from pious slogans to reality, we must be deliberately self-conscious of the *here*. The here-and-now derives meaning from, and imparts meaning to, the there-and-then. Any attempt to celebrate the one without regard for the other is an exercise in futility.

That, then, is the rationale behind the highly flexible Forms of Intercession. That is the here-and-now focus of the liturgy. Here-and-now is never exactly replicable. Furthermore, precisely because of its transitory nature, here-and-now demands the acceptance of responsibility. The Christian is not a passive spectator of history; he is an active agent in an on-going creation. In terms of the liturgy, his responsibility is translated into active participation in, and responsibility for, the Prayers of Intercession.

Responsibility is widely acclaimed as an abstract concept while being studiously avoided in actual practice. Most of us would feel much more comfortable if we could be handed an authorized text and instructed to pray those words, or, better yet, have them prayed for us. That, after all, has been our life-time custom. Some of us are going to be decidedly discomfited by the idea, not to say the practice, of actually assuming some responsibility for the corporate Prayers. Of course, it will still be possible for the officiating minister simply to read to us, with little or no forethought,

the form printed in the First Service. That, quite
obviously, is not the intention here. Even those forms
that lend themselves to recitation by a single voice,
punctuated only by a rote-type response on cue,
require a minimum of advance planning by the minister. Other forms, or the same ones used more
sensitively, call for varying degrees of preparation by
an indefinite number of participants. Even the mere
selection of the appropriate Form, its announcement
to the congregation, and decisions about the manner
in which it will be done, call for some choices to be
made prior to the beginning of the liturgy itself. Also,
there is no rubrical direction about posture. If it is
considered desirable for the entire congregation to
assume the same posture during the Prayers, a
decision will have to be made as to the one most
appropriate to the situation.

Decision-making and advance preparation are
not exactly common elements in the worship
experience of most Episcopalians (sadly, that holds
true for many clergy as well as for the laity). And yet,
many congregations who have been doing it for some
time have discovered that increased participation in
the Prayers and broader responsibility at this, and
other points, is productive of a greater sensitivity to
the liturgy as a whole. Once we get over the strange
feeling that results from being considered as persons
rather than as one of the "number of communicants
at this service," our worship will take on more meaning
in the here-and-now, and we will see more clearly
the relevance of the then-and-there. It will require
more forethought than we have been accustomed to

giving to an individual celebration, but it is to be hoped that every congregation will experiment as widely as the rites allow with various Forms of the Prayers and will discover thereby an even deeper appreciation of liturgical worship.

One of the chief functions of liturgical worship is to enable the People of God to exercise their royal priesthood. As successors to the Old Israel, we are God's "holy nation," his "kingdom of priests." The unique and distinctive function of a priest is to represent the people before God—not so much as their leader, but as one who acts on their behalf, vicariously. The priest gathers up the offering of the people, their alms, their prayers, their very lives, and lifts them up as the corporate offering, the common life, the great prayer. Like a kingdom of priests, the church works to do just that on behalf of all creation. That is what is meant by the phrase: "the priesthood of all believers." Christ is the Great High Priest, acting on behalf of all men. The Body of Christ, his church, continues his work through the ages.

It is fitting that we, acting as priests on behalf of the world, should actively and overtly participate in the work of the Prayers. Note that the rubrics specifically allow any member of the kingdom of priests to lead the Prayers of Intercession. In the First Service they are to be lead by the Deacon "or some other person appointed." The Second Service merely directs that "Prayer is offered . . ." The leader may be of either sex and of any age; the only requirement being the self-evident one of membership in the Body of Christ. Furthermore, there are no directions as to where the leader is to stand: sanctuary, choir, or nave. the primary consideration is one of audibility. The Prayers should originate from a place that they can easily be heard by everyone.

It should go without saying that the context of all Christian Prayer is the Body of Christ. The church's prayer is *the* prayer, and there is no other Christian prayer beside or in addition to the prayer of the church. Our private prayers have no existence of their own; they live only as part of the prayer of the church. That is why virtually all Christian prayers conclude with the words, "Through Jesus Christ," or some similar phrase. We pray as members of his Body; thus, we pray his prayer. Here, in the Prayer of Intercession, we do our work as a royal priesthood, joining the lives and the concerns of all mankind unto the acceptable offering of Christ.

In the order of printing in both the First and Second Services, the first part of our celebration is concluded by the exchange of the Peace. This may well be the oldest liturgical rite in the Christian tradition—it certainly is one of the most beautiful. As a conventional greeting, the word Peace had long been used by the Jews. But, as with so many of the riches inherited by the New Israel from the Old, its meaning ripened and came to full flower in the Christian context. "The Peace of the Lord" does not mean merely the absence of hostilities, and it certainly does not connote such a passive state as "repose." It is active and positive—and it is a gift. When Christian brothers exchange The Peace of the Lord, they are not simply wishing away one another's troubles. In fact, the Lord's Peace may well be a troublesome thing. At the same time that it conveys a blessing, it poses a challenge. It is The Peace of the Lord that at once enables and constrains us to pray. It is, therefore, most appropriate that we exchange the Peace at a point in the liturgy proximate to that of joining in the work of prayer.

Often we hear this liturgical action described as The Kiss of Peace. The word *kiss* simply describes the ceremony that customarily accompanied the exchange of greetings in many parts of the world—both ancient and modern. Even today we find that some peoples greet one another by a kiss on one cheek, or on both; others bow, slightly or profoundly. The American Indian would raise his right hand, palm outward. Much of the modern western world employs the ceremony of the handshake. The intent of all these various ceremonies is the same: to emphasize by a physical action the words that are being pronounced. The title Kiss of Peace is usually used as a generic term designating whatever ceremony might be employed. The word kiss, however, raises so many other connotations today that it is virtually useless as an inclusive term and has even become an over-used subject for tasteless jokes.

The trial-use rites wisely avoid reference to any particular ceremony in conjunction with the Peace; instead, we are given a helpful and welcome opportunity for experimentation. The literal requirement of the text may be satisfied by the officiant's verbal bestowal of the Peace upon the congregation as a whole and their corporate response. In many congregations such a brief exchange has been a part of liturgical worship for generations—although it may have occurred at a different place in the rite. For many, it will continue to be the preferred method.

On the other hand, it is becoming increasingly common among American congregations to engage in a more elaborate form of ceremony when exchanging the Peace. In most cases, this involves either a simple handshake or the clasping of both hands in some manner, or an embrace. The handclasp or embrace is usually given by the officiant to his assistants individually. They then pass the greeting to persons in the congregation who are standing conveniently near, each of whom turns to his nearest neighbor with the gesture and greeting. Every person then both receives and gives the Peace, passing it throughout the worshipping Body until all have personally and physically participated. With a little advance planning, such a ceremony can be accomplished quickly and with dignity.

The simple liturgical action can have great meaning for the participants individually and carry enormous significance for the community as a whole. It is both personal and corporate at the same time. It has an informality within a formal structure. The action is familiar and customary, and the words are simple; but, even so, they need not be considered invariable. Any phrase, such as: "The Peace of the Lord," or "Peace be with you," may be used. It is especially appropriate to use the Christian name of the person with whom one is exchanging the Peace, in such a manner as: "The Peace of the Lord be with you, Frances." "And with you, David." If one does not know his neighbor's name (unfortunately, a not infrequent experience in too many of our churches), he could simply ask. Would it be too much to expect that such a custom might eventually lead to our knowing the names of those with whom we break bread at the Lord's Table?

Someone has observed that if some such ceremonial does accompany the exchange of the Peace, it will be the one place in the entire liturgy where the individual is compelled to take part—it is the only act he cannot dodge. Hopefully, no one would want to avoid full participation in the celebration, but this enforced involvement, even performed with all brevity and formality, might be just the stimulus necessary to recall a wandering mind or activate a lethargic spirit. One fringe benefit that might accrue is that in uncrowded church houses we might be moved to gather more closely together, instead of trying to isolate ourselves by distance from our neighbors.

Despite the obvious preference expressed here for some form of ceremony to accompany the exchange of the Peace, it must be emphasized again that no particular ceremony of any kind is demanded by the rites themselves. Each congregation is free to devise, experiment with, and to develop the ceremony most expressive and most helpful to the people of God in that place and time. This flexibility will also enable the ceremonial expression of a congregation to change and grow as the congregation itself changes and grows. In fact, change and growth are two elements invariably concomitant to The Peace of the Lord.

## SUMMARY

Before proceeding to examine the details of the second part of the liturgy in the trial-use rites, it might be well to pause and take stock of where we have been and where we are at this point.

The Christian community has been called together. With a greeting and response, or some form of opening sentence, we have gathered in the Name of the Lord. Perhaps we have offered a prayer for our participation in the worship and have heard ourselves charged with the conditions of such worship. In any event, we have quickly raised our voices in praise of the One to whom worship is due.

Then, we heard the Word of God spoken to us today. The words themselves are out of our tradition and form our heritage. The Word is our identity and our life. By hearing (not merely listening) we are made to know that we are a people, the People of God, commissioned to carry out the ministry of Jesus Christ and to proclaim the imminent coming of His Kingdom. And we have responded by reaffirming our dependence upon the faith of the church.

Perhaps we have prepared for our celebration by participating in a service of penitence. If not, we now acknowledge the dependent nature of our creatureliness and the forgiveness of God that makes possible our very existence, not to mention our audacity in presuming to call upon His Name.

From that perspective, then, we dare to pray

for others and for ourselves, for the conditions and concerns that are most immediate to us. In so doing, we affirm ourselves and thereby witness to the glory that is God's.

Now, in the disturbing, challenging, yet somehow comforting Peace that *is* life in the Lord, we are able to greet our brothers in Christ. In fact, it is only in this context that we can really meet one another; we do so in His name.

Most celebrations build toward some expected climax: the presentation of a gift, a ceremonial toast, the cutting of the cake, the serving of the meal. The People of God, having gathered and greeted one another in the Name of the Lord, having adopted the agenda for their life together, now eagerly await such a climactic moment.

We are here!

We know who we are and why we live.

Let us break bread together.

Let the celebration continue!

# CHAPTER 3

# The First and Second Services—Continued

STRUCTURALLY, AT LEAST, the second part of the liturgy is virtually identical in all of the trial-use rites. In all that has gone before, each of the services has been distinguished by its own unique features and, in many cases, its own unique set of options with regard to the order in which the several component parts might be arranged. The first part of the liturgy is versatile enough to enable each celebration to be tailor-made for a specific situation, and this flexibility extends to the very structure itself as well as to the words and actions.

From here on, the variability, at least insofar as concerns the order of things, is noticeably curtailed. Although there are still a few decisions to be made about order, they are similar in the various rites and all of them are obviously peripheral to the main outline of action that now begins to stand out so sharply.

In contrast with the first part of the liturgy, variety in the second part is provided by means of alternate text for each of the sections rather than by options in the arrangement. From the Offertory Sentence to the conclusion of the liturgy, at least one alternate version is provided for every prayer or other spoken part in the Second Service. In the First Service, only one of the invariable prayers is left without an alternate text.

This flexibility represents a depature even from the LLS, and it marks an important contribution to liturgical worship. More significantly, it is an acknowledgement of a contemporary understanding of sacramental theology. For a good many years we have given lip-service (and there *is* a pun intended) to the fact that God's action in and through the sacraments does not depend upon the use of any specific verbal formulas. It is important, we have said, for us to rehearse certain things in a particular sequence. Furthermore, it is important for our language to reflect the best theological formulations of which we are capable. However, the importance of all this is to us, not to God, and the use of historic forms is for our protection, not because God is restricted in his action to any specific set of words. Still, in spite of our insistence upon the validity of such statements, we have tended to sacralize certain formulas and to treat them almost as objects of worship themselves.

Perhaps this tendency was first weakened by the obvious advantages of reading Holy Scripture in versions other than the traditional King James. Since then, the realization has grown that the important thing about our liturgical formularies was *what* they said and what we, as worshippers, perceived them to be saying, rather than the specific verbal forms in which they were couched. Theoretically, we have taken this stand ever since the Reformation, and the Roman Catholic Church has embraced it from the time of Vatican II. Now, we are beginning to translate our theory into practice, expressing our theology in a manner designed to communicate to modern man the basic and indispensible truths embodied in the traditional formulas. Inevitably, that means employing new verbal symbols as well as new constructions.

Furthermore, we have come to recognize the fact that no single liturgical rite can possibly present a complete and perfectly balanced theological statement. It is helpful, then, to have access to various texts—all saying essentially the same things, but each with its own emphasis and its unique nuances.

In spite of the variety of texts provided, however, there simply is no mistaking the intention common to all the rites—an intention reflected in, and dramatized by, a sequence and a structure that is clearly visible in each and that quite obviously forms the essential core of our eucharistic worship. We have been gathered, constituted, and commissioned. Now, there is a subtle but definite shift in the tone of the service. Through whichever of the optional routes we may have arrived at this point, we now converge. The object of our celebration becomes focused, and there is a marked quickening of the pace—now in a straight line. The action itself becomes paramount, and it proceeds in a deliberate, orderly fashion to its climax and then conclusion: the table is set, the meal is prepared, we give thanks. Then, we eat and drink—

the high point and the culmination of our celebration —and finally we are sent forth to be the Body of Christ in the world.

The shift in mood and pace is not jarringly abrupt. A transition is provided by the Offertory which summarizes and draws together all that has gone before and, at the same time, points toward that for which we have been preparing, anticipating what is yet to come.

Most of what has gone before might well have been led by someone other than a priest—the unique functions of priesthood being exercised by the congregation as a whole. Up until this time, the focal points have been the lectern, the pulpit, and the prayer desk. Now "The Priest, standing at the Holy Table, begins the Offertory." Performing transitional function, the Offertory redirects our attention several times before finally and naturally moving us to the next phase of our worship. First the priest, standing before the Holy Table on which the Offering will be presented, invites our participation. But the emphasis remains there only momentarily, shifting once again to the congregation and its representatives—from the altar to the choir and the nave. Then, finally and definitely, we are brought back to the altar. Now, there is increased intensity, so that we scarcely notice the point at which one act ends and the next one begins.

In keeping with the principle of directing only necessary ceremonial, the rites make no special provision for an Offertory Procession, although it is a commonly accepted practice and one that is seeing increased use throughout the Church. Briefly, the term Offertory Procession is used to describe an action in which representatives of the people, lay persons, bring up from the congregation not only the alms that have been gathered, but also the bread and the wine. Then, in full view of the people, the bread is placed on the plate from which it will be served and wine is poured into the cup. The symbolism of bringing these elements of bread and wine up from the congregation along with the alms is obvious. We have always been aware that these items were bought with the money we offered; but the practices of having them already on the altar, or on a small table beside the altar, and presented to the priest by an acolyte in vestments, and prepared in such a manner as to obstruct our view, have all tended to obscure our sense of participation in giving the bread and wine. Saint Augustine said that *we* are on the Altar in the bread; *our* blood is in the cup. When we offer these oblations, we offer ourselves. The eucharistic prayer states it all quite plainly, but the action of an Offertory Procession helps to make it more clear.

Here, again, there should be no distinction made of sex or age or office. Any member of the Body of Christ, any man, any woman, any child, may be appointed to represent the people in bringing forth the bread and wine. In many parishes, the custom has grown up of appointing one entire family— father, mother, children, even grandchildren—to represent the congregation each week. And certainly, if there is to be an Offertory Procession, there should be no thought of vestments.

The rubrics do make one ceremonial direction in this regard. Whoever brings forth the alms and the oblations should present them directly to the deacon or to the priest, rather than to an intermediating acolyte. The acolyte is, of course, a representative of the people, and he is a layman. However, his vestments and his office, again, tend to obscure that fact.

Occasionally the objection has been raised that an Offertory Procession seems to emphasize the wrong things—that it seems to be saying that *we* are offering something to God, out of the generosity of our hearts, whereas the true offering is his to us, made once and for all time by Christ. It certainly is true that "of thine own have we given thee." By himself, man can make no worthy offering. The offering, the sacrifice, is Christ's. Our unworthy offering is taken up by him, joined unto his perfect offering, and thereby *made* perfect, worthy, and acceptable unto God. But God does not wrest it from us—we have to proffer it. That is the symbolism intended by the Offertory Procession.

As mentioned earlier, however, there is no specific direction that there shall be an Offertory Procession. In certain situations, under a peculiar set of circumstances, it may be more desirable to have an acolyte, vested or not, bring the elements from a side table directly to the deacon or priest. This might be especially true at a small, midweekly service. In any event, *some* representative of the people is directed to perform this ceremony—the priest is not to do it by himself. If, at a midweek celebration, there is no acolyte present, the priest will ask some member of the congregation to come up and assist him with the preparation of the Table. As usual, neither sex nor age need be a consideration in the appointment of such a person.

Whether the ceremony be the simplest possible or highly elaborate, the entire community stands while the offerings are placed on the Altar. Standing at this point is another way of indicating corporate participation in the action and in the very elements of offering. According to our several abilities, we offer what we can. *We* are in the act of offering. *Our lives* are in the money and the bread and the wine. We stand as an indication of our individual involvement in the corporate act and in the collective offering.

At this point the new rites differ slightly from the LLS. While a variety of Offertory sentences are suggested (indeed, provision is made for the priest to use any sentence of Scripture appropriate to the occasion), there is no specific reference to a Presentation or to Presentation Sentences as such. Several of the suggested Offertory Sentences lend themselves well to such use, but their designation as such has been dropped; this was done in response to suggestions made after the first trial use period of the 1967 rite. It was noted by some respondents that the great eucharistic prayer that follows constitutes the Presentation proper and that the inclusion of so-called Presentation Sentences is premature and confusing. By omitting any reference here to "The Presentation" the Offertory becomes more obviously an integral part of the Great Thanksgiving.

The 1970 rites introduce the eucharistic prayer with a new title: The Great Thanksgiving. It is to be devoutly hoped that this will displace previous references to "the canon" and "the consecration." The word consecration has caused its share of grief in the church. Actually, it has the same root as the word sacred and means to set apart, or to dedicate to the service of the Lord. In practical use, we consecrate bishops and buildings as well as bread and wine. Novelist J. D. Salinger, in *Franny and Zooey,* says of the mother in his story that she serves to members of her family when they are ill "consecrated chicken broth"—in the context a perfectly legitimate use of the word.

But for many centuries, even unto our own, a favorite topic of controversy and conversation among theologians of all Christian persuasions has been precisely what elements constitute a proper or "valid" liturgical consecration and the sequence in which these often disputed elements must be arranged. In spite of a surprising unanimity of practice among Christians, disagreements over various details of the consecration have been among the principal *apparent* causes for the deplorable lack of visible unity in the Body of Christ.

As a title, Thanksgiving is vulnerable on the grounds that it is an inadequate description. Much more happens at this point than the giving of thanks. However, the word is merely an English translation of

the Greek term we render as eucharist, a title that has
been applied to this section of the liturgy, as well as
to the service as a whole, since the most ancient of
times. Thus it transcends, by virtue of its venerable
usage, the political and theological controversies that
have become associated with the word consecration.
Furthermore, if thanksgiving does not cover all the
action that takes place here, it is at least descriptive
of the attitude that pervades the whole.

The new rites make a far more significant
contribution than that of a new title, however felic-
itous; it lies in the quality as well as the variety of the
several texts provided. The First Service allows us to
choose from a slightly edited version of the prayer
as it appears in the 1928 book, a somewhat shorter
form of that same prayer, and the eucharistic prayer
from the LLS. The Second Service incorporates a
beautiful new prayer as well as the one from the LLS.
The only really new material introduced at this point
is printed in the text of the Second Service.

The 1928 prayer still has the familiar ring of
Elizabethan English. The 1967 version provides a
sort of transition from that to a more contemporary
manner of speech. In the new prayer of the Second
Service, the modern idiom comes into its own and we
have a formula thoroughly in keeping with the spirit
of the whole Second Service. In fact, it might be said
that each of the Services receives its tone or feel from
the central prayer chosen rather than vice-versa.

In actual use, one of the most noticeable features
of the new prayer is the incorporation of a congregational acclamation in the middle, with two alternate

forms of the acclamation provided in the final set of Directions and Suggestions. For too long now, the Great Thanksgiving prayer has been looked upon as exclusively the work of the priest. The prayer is relatively long, covering two full pages; it has been said entirely by the priest; and it has required no physical participation whatsoever from members of the congregation. In days gone by, it was almost invariably said with the priest's back to the people. Some parts were deliberately inaudible, and much of the rest was virtually so whether intended to be that way or not. Add to these impediments the fact that the priest may have recited precisely the same words every day for many years, and it is not surprising that it would be an unusual officiant who could make the great prayer sound at all vital and vibrant. Like-wise, it would be the unusual worshipper who, from his isolated position and posture, could feel any personal participation in one of the central acts of his worship.

In recent years several factors have begun to operate together to overcome this state of affairs. First has been the rapidly growing custom of placing the Holy Table in such a position that the priest can stand behind it, facing the people. That arrangement not only increases audibility to a marked degree, but also adds to the people's sense of participation by affording them the opportunity to see and focus upon the altar and the offerings spread upon it. That, in turn, has led many clergy to become more sensitive to the manner in which they read the prayer and to make a more conscious effort to communicate through it.

Another contributing factor has been the increasingly popular practice of standing at this point in the service. We have always stood for the Offertory, and now we are coming to see the eucharistic action as incorporating a ceremony for which we have always considered standing to be the appropriate attitude. The LLS directed us to stand until after the singing of "Holy, Holy, Holy," and many congregations have discovered the advantages of remaining in that posture of corporate participation throughout the remainder of the prayer. In *Is The Last Supper Finished?* Arthur A. Vogel explains some of the feeling behind this by likening the Holy Eucharist to a call from God to us. "Therefore," he says, "Christians stand during it to show, in the most obvious way possible, that they are there to answer God and make themselves available to him." At the Eucharist we stand to put ourselves at God's disposal.

Recently, suggested new forms of the eucharistic prayer and for prayers of all types have incorporated some audible participation by the entire congregation as a further indication of, and encouragement for, individual and corporate involvement in the act. The new prayer in the Second Service is an example.

It is not our intention to discuss here the Order that follows the two services; that will come in a subsequent chapter. However, it should be noted that the order provides four more eucharistic prayers. At present there is no specific rubrical direction for using one of them in either of the two Services. Probably the question would never arise in connection with the more traditional First Service as all four are obviously more suitable to a contemporary setting. However, any of them would fit quite naturally and helpfully into the Second Service. It does not seem to me that it would do violence to the spirit of the trial-use materials to utilize any of the additional prayers in the Second Service where their use seemed apposite. In fact, they could provide a welcome enrichment of our regular Sunday worship.

The Great Thanksgiving actually begins with the familiar salutation and response, followed by an invitation to "Lift up your hearts." The prayer itself opens with an acclamation of praise. On all Sundays and other Holy Days that opening incorporates a Proper Preface, which is simply a brief, variable introduction. The prefaces are important because they set the "special intentions" or the specific emphasis for the whole prayer. Each of the major seasons and events observed in the Church year has a special, or Proper, Preface.

In addition, we are given a choice of three Prefaces for use on regular Sundays. The first of them celebrates Creation, the second, the Resurrection, and the third emphasizes the work of the Holy Spirit in Baptism. This last is a particularly welcome addition as it is the one place where the eucharistic liturgy is obviously and explicitly tied to the primary sacrament of Baptism.

Following the Preface, the whole congregation joins in the great "Holy, Holy, Holy." This entire section is one glorious song; *Prayer Book Studies XVII* calls it "the greatest act of praise in all the liturgy . . . *eucharist* in the strictest sense." Need we add that it is to be entered into wholeheartedly, joyfully, exuberantly? Whatever our posture shall be for the remainder of the prayer, we are directed to stand and join in the magnificent anthem—not moaning the words from a fetal position, but upright and singing out with full and joyful voice.

As the Great Thanksgiving continues, allowance is made for the people to kneel; but note that the rubric here is permissive rather than directive. The people *may* kneel; but the people *may* remain standing as a symbol of their corporate participation and a sign of their role as cocelebrants with the priest and his assistants. (Technically, the wording of the rubric would allow any other posture as well; however, standing and kneeling are obviously the only postures appropriate to participation in such a laudatory and worshipful act.) Undoubtedly, the most widespread custom in the Episcopal Church today is to kneel for the prayer. Lately, as we mentioned before, the practice is being varied more and more. In any event, we now have rubrical provision for experimentation at this point.

Taking into account all the eucharistic prayers offered throughout the new materials, we find seven basic formularies, plus slightly modified versions of two of these—a total of nine possible forms. This profusion may take a little getting used to, but in practice should not prove to be at all confusing. In fact, it probably will afford a welcome variety that will override most other considerations. After all, we do not object to a variety of scripture readings. We welcome an opportunity to hear St. Luke's version of the nativity story just *because* it differs from that of St. Matthew and therefore adds another dimension. In fact, the several writers of the gospel story frequently present entirely different versions of the same events, and we find that enriching rather than confusing. The same attitude may be applied to the various texts used for the Great Thanksgiving.

There may be another unplanned-for but beneficial result. It will be less convenient, in many cases, for the congregation to follow the eucharistic prayer in their books. That is all to the good for, as in the case of Bible readings, the prayer is meant to be heard as it is spoken aloud. Perhaps the availability of different texts will encourage better reading on the one hand and more participatory listening on the other. Certainly, it should contribute to our experience of the Great Thanksgiving as an exciting adventure in prayer.

In any event, it should not prove difficult for anyone to follow the prayer, whichever of the versions is selected for use. All of them are based on a common outline. We begin with praise for God the Creator of all things and men, then acknowledge man's fall into sin. That is followed by a recitation of God's mighty act in Christ to effect our restoration and is highlighted by a recollection of the Last Supper, during which our Lord commanded us to "Do this in remembrance of me." Then, as we look forward in hope, we ask God's blessing upon ourselves and all that we do and offer in this celebration. The prayer concludes with a glorious doxology and a resounding "AMEN."

The Great Thanksgiving culminates in a unison recitation of the Lord's Prayer. In the Second Service, the text is that of the ICET, mentioned earlier in connection with the Creed. The ICET version should present no problem for most Churchmen as it is not really a very drastic, certainly not a radical, change. The difference will be immediately noticeable, however. For instance, we no longer have to worry about either the pronounciation or the meaning of "trespasses;" the proposed text straightforwardly says "sin." Most Americans are aware of two variations of the Lord's Prayer: one that uses trespasses, and the other that says debts and debtors. As one travels in other English speaking countries, he becomes aware of a number of other slight, but obvious, variations. Canon R. C. D. Jasper, Chairman of the Liturgical Commission of the Church of England, tells me that the response from his country has been overwhelmingly in favor of the principal of a common text for the Lord's Prayer because for the first time all Christians in the land will be saying the same version instead of the half dozen or more formerly used by different congregations there. A reaction more typical of American Episcopalians came from a friend who ironically complained that "now I have to really concentrate on what I'm praying." So be it.

The action that immediately follows the eucharistic prayer provides what is probably the most dramatic point in the liturgy—made so, perhaps, by its very simplicity and forthrightness. The bread is broken. Naturally. The bread *must* be broken. The one loaf is intended to be shared by all. From a purely pragmatic point of view, it must be broken in order that all may eat of it. In a more profound sense: only that which is first broken can be distributed among many. The Body of our Lord is broken for us— broken so that we might partake of it individually and share in it corporately. The Body of Christ— broken—that we might become, with him, with one another, with ourselves, One in the Body of Christ.

The full impact of the enormous significance in the act of breaking the consecrated bread is lost to us unless it is done in full view. The rubrics give no direction that the plain, powerful act must be performed in such a manner that all can see, but surely the fitness of doing so will be apparent to both priest and people. Much of the meaning is also obscured by the common practice of using individual sterile wafers for Communion. It obviously is *not* necessary, or even desirable, to break these; and somehow, breaking the seal on the package does not convey the same thing. We teach that we "share the one loaf"—but frequently we do not. Perhaps all those individual wafers were once part of a single sheet of dough rolled out on a counter before being cut and baked; but even if such a thought should ever occur to anyone, the idea is rather too remote to expect that it will carry any real significance.

So, we rationalize by saying that the "oneness" is symbolic. Each receives an identical wafer, in an exactly equal portion. The symbol hardly seems adequate to carry the fullness of what it is intended to symbolize, but if it *does* in fact do so, then well and good. Some congregations, no doubt experiencing a degree of difficulty in sustaining the symbolism of individual wafers, have begun to use larger loaves that have to be broken to be shared and have to be chewed to be eaten. Of course, there is a practical difficulty in the use of leavened bread: it does not keep as well as the unleavened wafers. Hence, a weekly purchase is necessary to assure a fresh supply —more trouble for the Altar Guild. If individual wafers are used, perhaps there could be more teaching and preaching done to explain the symbolism and its meaning. Perhaps only the large so-called "priest's hosts" could be used; these are simply a larger version of the smaller "people's wafers" which would require breaking for distribution.

In any event, the very fact that the rites here print a rubric requiring the breaking of the bread, and so title this section, will in itself help to convey some of the meaning that might otherwise have remained obscure. The simple, necessary act, so common, so obvious, is nevertheless fraught with significance. The consecrated bread, the Body of our Lord Jesus Christ is broken . . . for us. What can we say? Momentarily, nothing. And that is just what the rubrics call for: a period of silence to be kept. No response to the breaking of the bread could be more appropriate.

Silence does not mean organ music, even played quietly in the background. It means: not a sound. Silence in Church, which seems highly appropriate on the face of it, is an "awe-ful" thing. It is so powerful as to be downright threatening. After all, the Holy Spirit of God might actually speak. The very idea, not to mention the practice, is so frightening that wherever possible we purposely structure most of our worship in order to avoid silence as though it were a mortal sin. Before the service, after the service, at various intervals in the action during the service—where is there a period of real silence? In small congregations that cannot afford an organist, perhaps such a terrible fate may be forced upon us, but most manage to make some arrangements to fill the "void" with some noise.

The uneasiness will not be too apparent, however, at this point in the liturgy, for a period of silence is our natural and obviously apposite response. But it cannot, it must not, and it should not, last. Here our awe-inspired silence is broken by joyful song. Any fitting hymn or psalm may be used in this place, but the rites provide the text of an anthem which is both familiar and especially appropriate. And, except during the season of Lent, a great "Alleluia" may be used as an antiphon embracing the anthem itself. Again, the element of joyful, exuberant celebration. With a song in our hearts and a joyful noise upon our lips, we make ready to receive the Food of Heaven.

The priest then signifies to us that all is in readiness and that we are to gather around the Holy Table. We have arrived at the climax of our celebration! It is the epitome of all that we have been doing. This is what it has all been building up to, pointing toward. The focal point of all our worship

—indeed, of all our lives—is here, at this moment. It is both absolution and blessing, a foretaste of heaven, here and now.

Many congregations have found it meaningful to exchange the Peace at this point in the service, as they move forward to share the one loaf and the common cup with their brothers and sisters in Christ. As we receive the bread and wine, the priest or deacon reminds us of the nature of that which we eat and drink: the Body and Blood of our Lord Jesus Christ.

It will be noted that here, again, the rites have omitted any reference to the posture of the communicants. There is no requirement that we kneel to receive. The practice of standing to receive Communion has been observed by a large segment of Christendom for centuries. On the other hand, it is for the most part unknown in the Anglican tradition, and only very rarely was it seen in the American Episcopal Church until recently. Now, however, more experimentation in this matter undoubtedly will occur as a result of the trial-use rites because, in addition to the symbolism of standing which has already been discussed, there are some practical advantages to that posture.

In the first place, it is somewhat easier to administer a cup full of wine to one who is standing than to a person who is not only on his knees, but also usually behind a railing as well. Even more important is the possibility of speeding up the often quite prolonged act of administering bread and wine to a large congregation. By having the priest stand at one point, holding the plate with the bread, and placing another priest or a deacon beside him with the cup, the people can come in a constantly moving single line—first to receive the bread, then moving on to receive the wine. No one desires, of course, to *rush* the act of Communion or to speed through it at such a rate that the process seems more perfunctory than worshipful. Such a form of administration as we have described, however, can be done with dignity, without a sense of "hurrying through," and at the same time markedly reduce the time required to communicate several hundred people. In very large parishes, where several priests and deacons are available, more than one station for Communion might be established, thereby reducing the over-all time even further.

Whether we receive standing or kneeling, in a large congregation or in the company of only two or three of our brothers, we do so as members of the Body of Christ, feeding upon the Body of Christ. As we take his Body into our bodies, as his Blood passes our lips, our identity is established, our purpose fulfilled, and our celebration complete.

Having made Eucharist, in the fullest and deepest sense, and in a most graphic and expressive manner, all that remains is anticlimactic. That is not to say that the rest of the liturgy is unimportant, but simply to observe that anything that follows the highest and most significant action is, by definition, anticlimax. An effective liturgy is a dramatic form, and the rules of good drama demand that when the major turning point has been reached, the action move with all deliberate speed to a conclusion.

Up to the point of the communion, the liturgy has been building dramatically and theologically, at an ever-increasing tempo. Its direction has been up, aiming toward the obvious apex. Having attained that peak, the descent is dignified, even beautiful, but swift and purposeful. That which we were gathered to do has been done. That which we came to offer has been received. That which we came to receive has been bestowed. Anything that follows is bound to be redundant.

And so it is. Still, a certain amount of redundancy is necessary to order and dignity and good manners. Furthermore, it is not merely appropriate to the structure of the liturgy itself, it is necessary to the good ordering of our own minds and bodies and spirits. That is why the great Eucharistic act is not actually the conclusion of our celebration.

The First Service provides the familiar post-Communion thanksgiving prayer. That is, of course, just what we have been doing; but now it is a thanksgiving *after* the fact. We are giving thanks for the fact that we have been allowed and enabled to give thanks: a thanksgiving for Thanksgiving. The prayer may be said by priest and people together, following the custom already prevailing in many communities.

In the Second Service we have a choice between two brief prayers at this point: one is based upon the familiar thanksgiving but is considerably shortened; the other, somewhat more brief but obviously intending to say the same thing. Both, then, find their origin in the 1928 prayer, but the emphasis is shifted. In the original, the main theme is one of thanksgiving, followed by a request that we use the benefits of the communion just received to the glory of God. In the derivative forms in the Second Service, the emphasis is upon apostleship. We pray to be sent forth into the world to serve and to witness. Here, too, we find that priest and people are bidden to say the prayer together.

In the First Service the bishop, if he is present, or the priest, is directed to give us a blessing just before we are dispersed. The act is optional in the Second Service, and no text for it is actually provided. The final blessing was omitted from the LLS except when the bishop was present. That caused a great deal of consternation, probably due to a misunderstanding about the blessing itself. By any logic, a further blessing at this point seems superfluous. After all, we have just held the Body of our Lord and tasted His Blood. What further blessing could one ask? Many clergy had begun to feel that for them to add their blessing to the blessing of Christ was an impertinence. Still, it was missed by many people. One lady was heard to exclaim to her bishop that she was so glad for an episcopal visitation because "that's the only time we get blessed!" One gets the impression that she felt she received more benefit from the blessing than from the sacrament.

Whereas that lady, and others who feel as she does, are undoubtedly mistaken about the nature of the blessing, so are those clergy and people who view it as an impertinence. The blessing given is not the blessing of a particular man, it is the blessing of the church—hence, the direction that it should be given by the bishop whenever he is present. True, it may be a bit redundant here, but it surely is not wrong. As we have already seen, some ritual redundancy is a helpful thing. In effect, the blessing summarizes and concludes our liturgical act. None would deny that those of us who have participated in the eucharist are blessed—these words merely say so. They are based upon, and grow out of, our relationship with God in Christ—a relationship acted out in the liturgy and now spoken. True, they are not really essential to the celebration—this is why they are made optional in the Second Service—but neither are they inappropriate.

All that remains now is the dispersal itself, and several optional forms of dismissal are provided in each of the Services. It has been said that "the holiest moment in the liturgy is when the People of God, having been fed and formed by the Body of Christ, go out through the doors of the church to *be* the Body of Christ in the world." That is precisely the charge given us in the dismissal sentences. The liturgy, the people's work, is to be carried out and carried on. It finds meaning, content, and expression in the intervals between formal celebrations. A liturgical form that is completely contained within the confines of the church house is not, in any true sense, a liturgy at all. The church gathers and disperses and gathers and disperses in a never-ceasing round. It is rather like inhaling and exhaling: both are necessary components of the act of breathing. As the physical body lives by the continuing process of breathing, inhaling and exhaling, so the Body of Christ lives by the process of gathering and dispersing; liturgy becomes Liturgy becomes liturgy.

Thus, the celebration concludes on a note of expectancy rather than finality. This is no time to linger —this is the time to "Go forth!" Many parallels are often noted between the Lord's Supper and its precedent, the Passover Feast. In giving instructions for the Passover, God commanded: "Thus shall ye eat it; with your loins girded, your shoes on your feet, and your staff in your hand; and ye shall eat it in haste: it is the Lord's Passover" (Ex. 12:11). In like manner shall we eat of the Lord's Supper—with our shoes on our feet. The Eucharist is the sacrament of our journey. It would, of course, be much more comfortable to linger in the coolness and beauty of the sanctuary, protected from the world. The ancient Hebrews felt the same way; but had those feelings prevailed, they would still be in Egypt, and the Promised Land forever unattained. The Eucharist is the sacrament of life; and life means encounter with the world. We eat it with our shoes on our feet—enabled and made ready to live.

And we respond: "Thanks be to God!"

# CHAPTER 4

# *An Order for Celebration*

ONE HAS ONLY TO GLANCE at the "Order Of The Celebration," completely contained on two facing pages, to see the Shape of the Liturgy. If it provided no other benefits (and it does offer many others), the Order as printed gives us one of the best tools ever devised for teaching the principles and structure of eucharistic worship. Here, in bold outline, we can see what we are about when we engage in the liturgy of the Holy Eucharist.

In the way the Order is presented, one factor immediately stands out: the outline is based entirely upon *verbs!* People and priest together, making up the *laos,* the People of God, gather, proclaim and respond, pray, exchange, prepare, make, break, eat and drink. It is strikingly apparent that the Eucharist is something one *does.* The action is seen to be of primary importance. Because we are men and because we communicate chiefly through language, the words that accompany our action naturally play a significant role in our expression and in our understanding. But the words, with all their undeniable importance, are derivative, not normative. That is, the words are based upon the action—they grow out of it rather than govern it. The liturgy is not primarily an acting out of words; the words are there to explain, enrich, and enhance what we do. Our Lord said, *"Do* this in remembrance of me." He did not instruct us to recite any given set of words for the recalling of his Presence. The Order makes perfectly clear our intention to obey Jesus' command.

Never before have we had the benefit of so graphic a demonstration of the nature of liturgical worship. Looking at the Order, one can hardly help but be struck by the fact that it is indeed the structure of celebration. It is, of course, uniquely and obviously Christian in character and in content, but it is the prototype of all true celebration. After reading this Order for celebration, one is tempted to respond: "But of course; how else?"

On succeeding pages we will look more closely at some of the details and features of the Order, always bearing in mind that the several component parts are just that. Their significance lies only in their relation to the whole. It is much the same as knowing a person: one might examine thoroughly the particular details of a person's physical make-up, his intelligence, personality, or any other aspect; but we all recognize that our exerience of another person is the experience of a total human being. Actually, that is the approach we have attempted in our examination of the other eucharistic rites, and it is certainly as true for them as it is in this instance. The arrangement of the Order, however, makes our task much easier because the relationship of the parts to the whole is immediately apparent and the sustained awareness of that relationship is all but unavoidable.

After the title, the most arresting line of type in the Order is that which reads "The People and Priest." Punctuation marks are not used in connection with the headings that make up the basic outline; however, it is clear that they are elements of a sentence which, written in conventional form, would read: "The People and Priest gather in the Lord's Name, proclaim and respond to the Word of God, pray for the world . . . etc." Each of the clauses is one in a series of actions, and the subject of each is always "The People and Priest."

In other words, people and priest *together* perform each of the several acts and participate in the total liturgical action as discreet parts of a single acting subject. That is, in fact, the definition of community presupposed in the analogy of Body. St. Paul reminds us that the body is a single unit, indivisible, yet made up of individual, unique parts, each with its own function. Those several functions are, nevertheless, functions of the body, performed within and by the body and affecting the whole. Thus, each individual has his own role to play—the people as a whole has a distinctive role, and the priest has his role—but in each case it is the total Body, the *laos* that acts.

The liturgy, then, is not something done by the people alone, to which the priest is attached peripherally. Likewise, it is not something done by the priest while the people look on. It is an act of the *laos,* and every member of the Body—be he ordained or not—is a full member of that *laos.* The worshipping community is precisely that: a community, in the most profound sense of that word. The liturgical act is pre-eminently and inescapably a corporate act.

That is hardly a new idea. Nor is it a concept restricted to this particular Order. It has never been so explicitly stated, however, nor so obviously normative, in previous liturgical formularies. Here, each of the verbs clearly refers back to a common subject and, just as clearly, all of the components of that subject form a single unit. The community comes together to celebrate.

It is not just any community, however. "The People" refers quite evidently to the People of God. It is, then, the community of the baptized: "a chosen generation, a royal priesthood, a holy nation, a people claimed by God for his own." It is that common identity as the *laos,* as the Body of Christ, that enables the community to celebrate. Furthermore, that is *what* the community celebrates. God's mighty acts of creation and redemption are the occasion for, as well as the object of, the celebration.

The worshipping community gathers as the Body of Christ. That is the underlying meaning behind the phrase: "gather in the Lord's Name." We gather as a people created, formed, and redeemed by God in Christ. We respond in worship. We cannot create, form, or redeem ourselves; that has been done for us. And it is such great and glorious news that we can only celebrate.

It is appropriate for us to *say* that—not to remind God, not even simply to remind ourselves, but chiefly as a more or less formal declaration and acknowledgment of our identity. Man is a verbal creature. Thus, when we gather in the Lord's Name, it is important for us to say so, to declare ourselves, to state publicly who we are and what we are about. The People of God have come together to celebrate the living God and their common life in Christ—to worship the God who has bestowed such a munificent gift upon his creatures.

The celebration gets under way with the proclamation of, and response to the Word of God. The proclamation serves a manifold purpose. First, it makes explicit the creating and redeeming Word, thereby reinforcing our identity and helping to establish a perspective. Then, it makes that Word present for us in our here-and-now life situation. And the Word is applicable not only to the several individual lives of those gathered, but also to the common, corporate life of the community. Furthermore, the proclamation projects us into the future and beyond. The eternal significances of our present choices is radically reaffirmed.

The proclamation may take many forms. Certainly one essential form is the reading of the Story, or a portion of the Story. The Word of God is undeniably and inexhaustibly proclaimed in the gospel narratives, and that forms the paradigm for all proclamation. At the same time, the Word may be discerned under other forms as well. Other, even secular, resources are welcomed if they can help us to hear the living Word as it forms and informs all creation. While reading from the Gospel is directed as being indispensible, no other media are explicitly denied. The only criterion is that through whatever forms are employed, the Word of God may be heard speaking and acting.

Thus, the forms for proclamation must be more than effective media of communication; they must convey a particular content. While McLuhan has hold of an important truth when he asserts that the medium *is* the message, it is an over-statement to say that the medium can convey only its own message. The medium may have much to say in and for itself, and surely it will color the communication; but without a substantial body of content it is a hollow and impotent thing.

Forms for proclamation, then, must be chosen not on the basis of their potential ability to communicate *anything in general,* but for their viability as communicative agents for *something in particular:* namely, the saving Word. Unless that single criterion is strictly observed, virtually any means of communication can be reduced to the level of entertainment alone. There is nothing wrong with entertainment, but the purpose of the proclamation is not to entertain but to confront, convict, affirm, challenge, and change —in short to *save.*

Just as the proclamation might be made in a variety of ways, so our individual and corporate responses may vary. Just how (that is, in what manner) we respond will depend upon many factors. Our response will be determined by what we have heard,

how we have perceived the Word and how we interpret the significance of the proclamation. It will
depend a good deal upon habit of communication and
cultural influence—that is, how we have learned from
experience to communicate. It will be governed by our
own tastes and our feeling of what constitutes an appropriate form of response to the Word. And, finally,
our range of possible responses will be limited by our
capabilities. Different groups will habitually turn to
different modes of response. Furthermore, the same
groups will vary their response according to differing
circumstances and occasions.

Again, the emphasis is not upon the form our
response takes, but upon the adequacy and appositeness of whatever form is selected. The forms may
range from total, contemplative, reflective silence to
dance—from small discussion groups to congregational singing—from individual self-expression
through the plastic arts to corporate expression in a
litany. In any event, we have gathered in the Lord's
Name to hear the Word of God, and our immediate
response is only a prelude to an even deeper form of
response to follow.

Part of the business of the royal priesthood, if
not its sole function, is to lift up the world-community
to God, to offer on behalf of the world what it cannot
or will not offer for itself—if only because it does not
know how or to whom. Secure now in our own identity
as the People of God, we turn to that business with
confidence and hope.

Elsewhere in the new eucharistic formularies (in

the Appendix discussed earlier on pages 68–74) we are provided with a number of suggested forms for intercessory prayer. Any of these may, of course, be employed at this place; however, the Order does not specifically direct that we shall be bound by any of the printed texts. We are free to construct our own prayers for the world and the church. Under most circumstances, we would do well to follow more or less carefully the outline provided in the Second Service. The chief benefit of a guide such as this is to serve as a reminder of the vast range of concerns appropriate to Christian worship. At the same time, in situations that call for the use of this Order, it is perhaps even more important than in the more formal services to build the prayer around the immediate concerns of the particular worshipping community and its various members.

There is much discussion today about the development of forms of prayer that are authentic expressions of twentieth-century men. Usually such discussions center around individual prayer, but all individual prayer by Christians grows out of, and is fed by, the corporate prayer of the liturgy and, in turn informs and feeds the liturgical expression. Quite properly, we have felt a good deal more freedom to experiment with individual prayer; but if such experiments are truly to be helpful, they must find their counterparts in our corporate prayer. The way is now open to us to experiment in this area. We are not constrained to devise prayer forms appropriate to all occasions or to all congregations of Christian worshippers. We already have a selection of prayers designed to meet the more general requirements of the church. Our prayers, then, may speak only for us, at this particular time and in this unique situation. They may never again be formulated in precisely the same way. Here, as before, the emphasis is upon the act of prayer rather than upon the specific words—upon the content rather than the medium.

After the prayers, we exchange the Peace with one another. Probably enough has been said about the significance of that act of eucharistic celebration. Many of the occasions calling for the use of the Order will involve a relatively small number of people. In such instances, the exchange of the Peace probably will be highly informal and it may well be that every member of the community will have an opportunity to exchange the Peace personally with every other member. The Peace may be literally "exchanged" rather than "passed," as must of necessity be the case in many larger or more formal gatherings.

In the Order we see even more clearly than before that the responsibility of preparing the Table and furnishing the Offerings belongs to the *laos* as a whole. Frequently in such celebrations, the Table is brought out to the center from against a wall where it has been previously, or even from another room. Various members of the community help spread the cloth and place the elements of Offering and the necessary vessels for their distribution.

The pattern of our worship has been exactly the same as it was for the Services, but perhaps that basic outline has been more highly visible. In any event, with the setting of the Table, our celebration approaches its climax as we gather around for the Great Thanksgiving.

Specific forms are provided for the offering of the Great Thanksgiving. As we mentioned earlier, a wide variety of types and styles are provided for our selection. Four of them are printed immediately following the outline of the Order. In addition, any of the eucharistic prayers furnished in the First and Second Services may be used.

Specific texts are directed for several reasons. Many clergy simply do not feel adequate to compose a sufficiently balanced eucharistic prayer. After all, they have had virtually no experience or training in such a thing, having always used formularies written and authorized by official bodies of the Church. Furthermore, many lay people share their viewpoint and do not feel confident that their clergy are theologically (not to say literarily) competent to do this on their own. In order to put both the people and the priest at ease during this important moment, authorized texts are provided. The choice is so broad, and the styles so varied, that one or more of them is virtually certain to fit quite naturally into almost any occasion of worship.

In many of the Great Thanksgivings the people participate audibly at several points. The intent is that they will participate on an even deeper level at all points. That intent is made explicit by the direction that, no matter which prayer is used, "The People respond—Amen!" The use of the exclamation point is not simply grammatical.

Finally, climactically, the Bread is broken and "The Body and Blood of the Lord are shared." The only ceremonial direction at this point is that the crucial action be done in a reverent manner. Just who passes what to whom and what words, if any, are said to accompany the act is left up to the discretion of those planning and conducting the worship.

Likewise, there are no directions given for a dismissal following the consummation of the consecrated elements. It is to be assumed that any community as close as this one has been—or, as a result of sharing this experience, has become—will find an appropriate manner of departing. It could take the form of maintaining silence while each of the participants goes off to bed after a celebration culminating a day of common endeavor. It might be a hearty round of applause, or singing, or dancing. On the other hand, it might be that the celebration does not mark the conclusion of their time together, but the beginning. For instance, they might then sit down together for a meal or a time of study or some other activity. In that event, there will perhaps be no dismissal or leave-taking at all. Whatever the circumstances, an appropriate response is to grow out of the community experience, not to be imposed upon it.

All of the foregoing seems to call for a degree of commitment, sophistication, and involvement far exceeding the liturgical experience of most Churchmen. Precisely so. It is for just that reason that the title page of the Order states quite clearly that the form is proposed for use "on occasions other than the principal service on Sundays and other feasts of our Lord." It is, instead, intended for use by communities with the time and the resources to apply to careful preparation on the part of all who are to participate. The Introduction to *Prayer Book Studies 21* states forcefully:

> "It cannot be stressed too strongly that this Order is not intended to displace the regular celebration of the authorized complete rites. It would be a gross travesty were a priest and a few acolytes to prepare the celebration in accordance with this Order, and then spring it on an unprepared congregation."

The entire rationale for the Order, along with a consideration of many of the occasions upon which its use would be most appropriate, is put forth so well in the Study that we can only refer the reader to that document if he still remains unconvinced of the need for such an Order or confused about the role it might play in the liturgical life of the Church.

We can, however, add one point. One who has participated in the preparation and celebration of such a liturgical expression as this will surely experience an enrichment in his appreciation of all Christian liturgy. He will be forced to examine some of his presuppositions about worship and about his responsibility to his fellow worshippers in this community enterprise. He will be free to face honestly his own commitment. He will begin to discern meaning where before there might have been confusion or mere apathy. He will begin to understand some of the potential of the eucharistic life.

Even more importantly, one who has had the experience of preparing and participating in a celebration such as this will have tasted what it is to *belong* to a community, as opposed to simply being a member of a congregation. It is a costly experience—a risky business—to share with one's brothers and sisters the most important things in the world. At the same time, it is a thrilling and joy-filled adventure. It is, in fact, something worth celebrating!

# CHAPTER 5

# Making Use of Trial Use

ON VIRTUALLY EVERY PAGE of the new rites, not merely in the Order of the Celebration, we have discovered at least one, often several, choices to be made and decisions to be arrived at prior to the service. These have involved everything from simple directions about posture to the composition of prayers. They have ranged from basic decisions about the structure of the rite to the choice of texts. On top of that, there are many more decisions implied: the use of architectural space, arrangement of furniture, decorations, selection of music, even such things as the time and frequency of services and the choice of what kind of bread is to be used and who is to supply it.

Who will make all these decisions. Whose responsibility is it? Whose celebration is it?

In 1967, when *The Liturgy of the Lord's Supper* was authorized for trial use, the Standing Liturgical Commission issued a set of guidelines that strongly recommended the establishment of a liturgical committee in every parish, mission, and other worshipping congregation. It was envisioned that such a parochial committee would embark upon a study of liturgical worship in general. Further, it was hoped that they would consider the various options and variations offered in the LLS, arrange for some experimentation with each of them, and participate in the decisions about how and when such experiments would be conducted.

Many parishes followed the suggestion and established such committees. Naturally, they functioned with greater or lesser degrees of success, depending upon many factors. Quite a few of them, unfortunately, found themselves primarily occupied with the distribution, collection, and tabulation of the questionnaires concerning the LLS. When that project had been completed, they ceased to exist.

Now, there is more need than ever for the establishment of such groups within every worshipping community, and for reasons that have nothing to do with questionnaires. Still, many congregations are uncertain about the role and even the constituency of a parochial committee on worship.

Hopefully—certainly—we are emerging from a long period of clerical domination of the liturgy. Characteristically, the manner and even the occasions of community worship have been determined by the clergy. At the same time, the clergy have consistently and passionately preached the gospel of lay participation and have been puzzled and frustrated by the lack of response. Finally, we are coming to realize—in fact as well as in theory—that the liturgy is not the priest's service. It is a celebration by the *laos*. As a member of that *laos* who has been chosen to perform a special function within it, the priest has a valuable contribution to make to the community's worship. But the people have a responsibility for, and a contribution to, that worship which is at least equal to that of the priest. It is part of his function to teach and to lead. It is not any part of his role to exercise exclusive control over the liturgy.

But a vicious circle has been created. Long years of inexperience in liturgical matters have left the people feeling totally incompetent to make substantive decisions about their worship. In fact, denied the right to speak authoritatively in that holy realm, most of them have seen little point in bothering to learn very much about it or even to think about it at any real depth. And the less they knew, and the less they felt adequate to discuss the subject, the less influence they were able or willing to bring to bear. Decreased influence led to even less involvement, less knowledge, and still less confidence. And so it went.

In recent years, however, people have begun to learn about celebration from sources other than the church. The study of psychology and sociology, an increased contact with and exchange between various ethnic groups, and the rise of a "youth culture," have all contributed to a resurgence of interest in liturgical celebration. At the same time, the clergyman has come to realize that he may not, after all, be "the expert" in the art of celebrating. He has been learning along with the people, and from many of the same sources.

It is high time that priest and people learned together to celebrate together. That is the chief function of a parochial liturgical committee. It should be open to all who are interested, but definitely should include representatives of all segments of the community. Its membership should be drawn from the vestry, the choir, the Altar Guild, and the Church School teachers; but it should also include representatives of the youth groups, young married couples and single persons, as well as the older members of the congregation. It would be well if at least one or two members could be recent converts and another one or two be recent transfers from another city. The point is that while any group might easily grow so large as to become unwieldy, it should at the same time be of sufficient size to include the valuable contributions of a wide variety of interests and ages. If the group became too large for profitable discussion, it might be divided into various subcommittees for particular studies and discussion, convening as a committee-as-a-whole for important decision-making.

Naturally, the clergy should be members of any such committee. They have a certain specialized knowledge and have developed certain skills that are invaluable to any group studying worship. Furthermore, they have an indispensable role to play in the liturgy itself. But they should be *members* of the committee. It should not be allowed to become a rubber-stamp for the rector's decisions or to degenerate into a school of liturgics taught by the clergy.

The period of trial use can be a time of frustration and confusion. Or, it can be a time of excitement, discovery, and growth. But there are innumerable decisions to be made. These decisions have to be communicated to the congregation. The materials, and even the concepts, need to be interpreted. And then someone needs to be able to hear and be sensitive to the congregational response, and to interpret that response. It is simply unrealistic to expect that all this, or even most of it, can be done effectively by the clergy alone. It is irresponsible of the community either to ask them to do it or to allow them to.

In the formation of a parochial liturgical committee there are several resources available. The most proximate of these is the Chariman of the diocesan liturgical committee. He, in turn, should be able to suggest additional sources of help. One of the most experienced and helpful resources in this area is an organization known as The Associated Parishes For Liturgy and Mission. They have established a network of liturgical consultants or advisors throughout the country who can make suggestions, supply material resources, or even conduct brief workshops for liturgical committees. Information about help they might be able to supply may be obtained by writing to the Executive Secretary, P.O. Box 74, Washington, Connecticut 06793.

In most parishes, however, the chief resource will be found to be the worshipping community itself. Some outside aid may be desirable in the form of advice, initial guidance, or expert knowledge from time to time; but all that will be most helpful when it is consciously directed toward the purpose of developing the potential for meaningful worship that already exists in most Christian congregations. Given a little encouragement, almost any worshipping community will soon discover that it really does know something about celebration and that it has something to celebrate. One thing worth celebrating might well be this very discovery!

# A Personal Postscript

"The sleeping giant."
"God's frozen people."
"The via media."

Over the years many phrases have been constructed to describe (in terms complimentary and otherwise) the Episcopal Church. Not all are as striking as those by Billy Sunday, Mark Gibbs, and George Herbert, noted above. Probably the most frequently used characterizations by those who are not Episcopalians themselves refer to our forms of worship: "the worshipping church," or, by the more sophisticated, "the liturgical church." The Episcopal Church is referred to by other Protestants, and even by non-Christians, as "high," meaning, quite likely, "their worship is like the Roman Catholics."

In a way it is rather strange that Episcopalians should be known chiefly, if not exclusively, for the way they worship. Episcopalians are not the only ones who "worship in spirit and in truth." Certainly we do not worship more *frequently* than other Christians. In fact, most statistics put us rather far down on the list of "frequency of worship," behind Roman

Catholics, Baptists, and several other traditions. It cannot be that Episcopalians characteristically talk about their worship outside of Church; it is more common to find them reticent to discuss even the fact of their worship, must less the form of it. Nor is it true that the Episcopal Church is the only one that has a regular, ordered liturgy for the celebration of Holy Communion; Roman Catholics, Lutherans, members of The Christian Church, and others participate in a eucharistic liturgy at least weekly. Furthermore, one may be sure that other Christians are not inclined to concede that Episcopalians have a better or truer liturgy than they.

Yet, in speaking of the Episcopal Church, the first thing that is apt to come to one's mind is some reference to the manner of worship, even if the speaker has never attended an Episcopal service. Whether such ascriptions are accurate or imagined, uttered in admiration or derision, they make inescapable the conclusion that the most preeminent feature of our Church is her worship. Other Churches might be known for their fervent evangelism or for their zeal in promoting and supporting work in the foreign or domestic missionary fields. Still others might be noted chiefly for a particular moral stance or for a distinctive theological position. Some Churches are renowned for their methods of Christian Education, some for the strong bond of fellowship that exists among their members. While the Episcopal Church has all those features to some degree, they do not seem to be paramount.

As an institution, she has never sought nor held

political power. With certain notable exceptions, she has not been a leader in social reform. Almost no one associates the Episcopal Church with any particular theological position—indeed, the very idea of theology scares most Episcopalians to death. (That is apparent in the use of the adjective "high" to describe the Church; originally the term indicated a definite theological stance, but today virtually its only connotation has to do with worship.) Although the Episcopal Church had long been in the forefront of the ecumenical movement, only a few are aware of her significant contributions in this area.

Whatever else she may be or may have to offer, the Episcopal Church is thought of first as "the worshipping Church"—"the liturgical Church." Such a description refers not only to a peculiar manner of worship, although it includes that, but also to the Church's interest in and emphasis upon that particular form of worship.

Furthermore, that viewpoint is shared by most Episcopalians themselves. Many were attracted to this particular denomination by the way of worship. For others, it is the principal, if not the only, reason they remain within the Episcopal fold. That is not to say that her peculiar form of worship is universally attractive; there are many others who are repelled by it and some who go so far as to say that they would really like to become Episcopalians but cannot bring themselves to do so because of the worship. Even that, however, is an acknowledgment of the centrality of liturgical worship in the Episcopal Church.

Most Episcopalians would have to say that, for

them, their worship *is* their experience of the Church and vice-versa. Of course, they would then acknowledge all sorts of other aspects of the Church's life and work, but all those stem from, are nourished by, and finally return to, the act of worship. The hours we spend in worship are, in fact, just about the only contact most of us ever have with the entity called "The Episcopal Church." Everything else the Church does or is takes its meaning from the worship. The attitude of the rest of the world, then, derives from, and finds confirmation in, our own attitude.

Many, inside and outside the Church, consider the Prayer Book to be the cornerstone of the Episcopal Church: "it is what holds us together." (Those who say that are correct in a certain sense, but often not in the sense, or to the degree they believe. As a unifying agent, *The Book of Common Prayer* is more of a symbol of unity than an instrument.) Methodists may seek their identity in, and derive their theology from, their Hymnal; Baptists may use the Bible for the same purpose; but Episcopalians know who they are and what they believe because of the Prayer Book.

Willy-nilly, then, and for good and evil, the Episcopal Church *is* the worshipping Church, at least among the non-Roman Catholic bodies. The role has been granted her by other Christians, acknowledged by non-Christians, and eagerly (if not always humbly) assumed by Episcopalians. But it is a role that carries with it mixed blessings: awesome responsibilities as well as certain privileges of status, vexing problems to plague the pleasures, and heavy burdens that threaten to spoil the satisfactions.

Naturally, given her role, the Episcopal Church is expected to take the leadership in developing liturgical forms. She is looked to as *the* liturgical expert outside of Rome. In her ecumenical encounters, her chief contribution is not seen to be any particular theological insights, nor a specific social concern, nor even "apostolic succession." Rather, she is thought of primarily as the chief resource on matters of worship and liturgy.

There was a time, just a few years ago, when the role of the Episcopal Church as the liturgical Church was in danger. It wasn't that others were challenging her or seeking to wrest the position for themselves. Nor was it that she was getting tired and gradually sinking into retirement. It was even more dangerous than that: she had begun to believe her own publicity. She had become so proficient in one aspect of worship that she concentrated all her attention on preservation and had forgotten how to grow. She was in danger of becoming like the man with one talent: it was unquestionably precious, so she wrapped it in a napkin (admittedly a beautiful one of silk-damask) and buried it in the ground. She erected a gothic tombstone over it and *almost* succumbed to the temptation to worship its memory!

Within her own house, the peculiar ethos that characterizes the Episcopal Church led her to seek answers for all her own problems, as well as those of the world, in the liturgy of the Prayer Book. When the problems proved to be recalcitrant, she *almost* fell into the trap of blaming, or ignoring, the problems.

In both cases, we have said "almost"—and it

was almost, but not quite. Now, slowly, tentatively at first but with a growing confidence and an increasing sense of responsibility and mission, the Episcopal Church has begun to arouse herself from her liturgical lethargy.

This book records one of the early steps in the "getting up" exercises. The rites authorized for trial use in 1970 certainly are not the end of the day. There are other whole sets of muscles that haven't even begun to come awake as yet. And even when we have them all toned, the rigors of the day's activities will demand constant testing and flexing and adaptation. But at least we've heard the alarm; we're out of bed and eager to face the world. The worshipping Church is emerging from the sacristy, "singing and making melody to the Lord!"